AF471082

PILLGWENLLY : NEWPORT

Volume One

First Edition 1983

© The Starling Press Ltd

ISBN 0 903434 85 7

This book is published by The Starling Press Ltd
in collaboration with Newport Borough Council.

Printed and Published in Great Britain by The Starling Press Ltd
Risca Newport Gwent NP1 6YB South Wales

PILLGWENLLY : NEWPORT

Cliff V Knight

THE STARLING PRESS LTD
Printers & Publishers
RISCA NEWPORT GWENT
GREAT BRITAIN
1983

DEDICATION
To the Residents of Pillgwenlly
Past & Present

Foreword: Councillor Harry Jones
Chairman of Newport Housing Committee

When Mr C V Knight retired in 1982, after many years of service with the Borough Council, everyone recognised that his knowledge of the people and history of the Pillgwenlly area would be irreplaceable. The Housing Committee therefore decided to sponsor Mr Knight in the production of a document cataloguing significant events in the re-development of Pill. From that modest aim a major piece of social research has emerged. Volume 1 traces the changes of Victorian times. Future volumes will bring us right up to modern times. As Chairman of the Housing Committee I am looking forward particularly to the history of the 1960s and 70s when deterioration and declaration of Housing Action Areas occurred. It is a period of massive Council investment, of successes and mistakes, which holds lessons for all who build houses and all who live in them.

I congratulate Mr Knight on his achievement and hope that this book will be of interest not only to the people of Pill but to all the residents of Newport.

The Author Thanks

1 Councillor Harry Jones, Chairman of the Newport Housing Committee and Mr John Bader, Director of Housing who suggested that this book be compiled, and for their subsequent help and encouragement.

2 Newport Borough Council for their ready support and co-operation.

3 All who have helped to compile this book (especially the residents of Pillgwenlly) by supplying information, granting interviews, and loaning and donating photographs. (The names are too many to mention individually.)

4 The Staff of the Newport Reference Library also the staff of Cardiff Reference Library.

5 Mr Alf Ropke, Director of Leisure Services, and the Staff of Newport Museum & Art Gallery.

6 The Rev Graham Harrison, MA, BLitt, Minister of Emmanuel Evangelical Church, Pill, for reading the script.

7 Mr Allan Parry, BEd, Art Master, Bassaleg Comprehensive School who supplied the sketches.

8 Viv Sugar, Support Services Manager of the Housing Department for her interest and support.

9 Susan Bale of the Housing Department who did all the typing.

10 Mr F E A Yates, Managing Director & Publisher in Chief, The Starling Press Ltd for his invaluable and friendly advice.

11 The *South Wales Argus* for some of the photographs which appear and for the publicity given in April 1982 when it was decided to compile this book, and the subsequent publicity.

12 Mr Jan Preece of Capel Friar Photography who took many photographs for the Pillgwenlly Redevelopment Advice Centre, some of which are reproduced.

The Author—C V Knight

Profile of Cliff Knight

In 1972 Cliff Knight was placed in charge of the Pillgwenlly Redevelopment Advice Centre to advise all who requested help. Many local residents quickly recognised that Cliff Knight was a person admirably suited to this task; he himself had been born in Pillgwenlly in 1919 so he knows the district well. He had attended Alexandra School, and later, St. Julian's High School. His first job was as a clerk at the Transporter Bridge until he joined the 5th British Infantry Division on the outbreak of World War Two in 1939. His Army service took him to France, Holland, Belgium, Norway, Ireland, India, Italy, Sicily, and the Middle East. As a Sergeant in the Royal Army Medical Corps he took part in the invasions effected at Sicily, then Italy and soon afterwards at the famous Anzio beachhead.

On demobilisation he was employed in the Planning Department at Newport's Civic Centre before he was posted to the Advice Centre until 1982 when the redevelopment was completed.

Cliff Knight for over fifty years has been associated with the Alma Street Baptist Church now known as Emmanuel Evangelical. He is an Elder, Deacon as well as Editor of the GAZETTE, the church magazine. A widower—his wife Nancy (née Luxton) died five years ago—he has a married daughter living in North Wales. Mrs Ceridwen Ruth Williams, with her husband Idris, Iwan (4) and Owain (2). Idris' father is the Welsh actor in Pobol y Cwm, Charles Williams, recently honoured with the MBE, and winner of the 1983 'Welsh Oscar'.

During his ensuing retirement in 1982 he was requested by the Newport Council to call on his experiences and reminiscences, in order to write a history of this Pillgwenlly area. He completed this voluntary task then visited me to discuss possibility of publication. We have had many cordial discussions, and a few serious moments, which culminated in our visit to the office of the Director of Housing, Mr D J Bader, one of the Newport Council's chief enthusiasts who encouraged this project. The result of our joint discussions will ensure that Cliff Knight's unselfish endeavours in researching and writing will have a permanent record. In partnership with the Borough of Newport, The Starling Press Ltd has now published this Volume One of PILLGWENLLY: NEWPORT and we are delighted with the response from this Council as well as from the residents of Pill. It is planned to continue with the account by publishing Volume Two to include material left out of the first book in order that the retail price of each copy be within the reach of the local residents.

F E A YATES
Managing Director & Publisher in Chief
The Starling Press Ltd

Contents

1 Diary of Events 1800 to 1875 9

2 Introduction 55

3 Early Transport 58

4 Churches and other Religious Communities 61

5 The Cattle Market 85

6 Coronation & Belle Vue Parks 87

7 The Schools 90

8 Some Old Traditions, Street Life and Recollections ... 93

9 The Transporter Bridge 98

10 Street Names 101

11 The Old Town Dock and the Alexandra Dock... ... 104

12 Some Well-known Personalities 107

13 Sport 117

14 Festivals and Carnivals, 1974-76... 122

15 Pill Branch Library, Temple Street 123

16 Index 125

17 Sources of Information 131

18 "Pillgwenlly" Newport—Vol II 133

19 Photograph Sections at rear of book

Publisher's Note

Reproduction of some of the photographs has been impaired due to age. They are included however since it is important to have them as historical records. The reader is requested to make allowances when bearing this in mind, since the Printers have attempted to overcome this difficulty. Blurred images and variations in tone are due to faulty photographs and are not the product of printing inadequacies.

1. Diary of Events 1800 to 1875

1800

Pillgwenlly uninhabited marshland.

1805

Extension of Monmouthshire Canal from Town Wharf (just south of Newport Bridge) to Pill agreed.

1806

Death of first Sir Charles Morgan (succeeded by his son).

1807

Lease granted to Tredegar Wharf Company by Sir Charles Morgan to construct Commercial Road (Pill Road).

Tredegar Wharf Company acquire 200 acres of land at Pillgwenlly.

1810

Commercial Road constructed.

Extension of canal commenced.

1812

Extension of Canal Completed.

New Cardiff Road (called "Street") formed.

Salutation Inn at the junction of Cardiff Road and Commercial Road built.

1817

Union Inn, Canal Side, Jacks Pill built.

1827

Mariners' Chapel, Canal Side (north of Jacks Pill) opened. (First Chapel of its kind in Great Britain.)

1829

Welsh Calvinistic Chapel (Ebenezer) built at the junction of Commercial Road and Ebenezer Terrace. Opened 1 November 1829.

Much shipping activity along Riverside Wharves. Main imports include sheep, pigs, cattle, slates, timber, cider, oats, potatoes. Exports consist mainly of coal and iron.

Conditions of working people (labourers) worse than they have been for some time. Attributed to number of Irish immigrants who come daily by Steam Packets from Bristol. Men, women and children for the most part seen on the streets without shoes and stockings, begging at shops and houses and applying for overseer's relief.

High tides cover much of the Pillgwenlly area. Many wharves damaged. Tredegar Wharf (near Pill Gates) completely ruined.

Pillgwenlly referred to as "being near Newport".

Punishment for crime severe. Man given two months imprisonment with hard labour for stealing coal from Thos Prothero's Yard (near Pill Gates).

Annual Cattle Show under the patronage of Sir Charles Morgan held at Court-y-Bella Farm.

1830

Coal miners' strike in Monmouthshire affects export of coal from Pillgwenlly. Miners' wages being reduced by 2d per ton.

Arrangements being made to adapt tramroads for locomotive engines to replace horses.

Locomotive engines used to transport coal from collieries to wharves in Pillwgenlly.

1831

Project for constructing floating dock (Old Town Dock) entertained. Estimated cost £60,000.

1832

Pillgwenlly Wesleyan Chapel built near "Pill Gates", Commercial Road.

Cholera epidemic reaches Pill. Master of ship from Cork dies.

Sir Charles Morgan's Annual Cattle Show at Court-y-Bella Farm. Much interest from surrounding counties.

1833

Salutation Inn, Commercial Road, used by Conservative Party.

Sir Charles Morgan's Annual Cattle Show at Court-y-Bella Farm well patronised.

1834

New ships launched at John Young's Shipbuilding Yard near Dock Parade and at Mr Perkins' Yard near Jacks Pill.

Disastrous fire at the stables of Thomas Phillips.

1835

Meeting to discuss "Newport Floating Dock" (Town Dock) held at the King's Head Hotel.

Newport Docks Bill passes all stages in Parliament.

Construction of Town Dock commenced. Two year contract granted to Dike and Meyrick of Bristol.

Joseph Latch, Pill Businessman, elected first Mayor.

1836

Brig "Jane Hunt" launched from Mr Perkins' Yard.

Schooner "Harmony" launched from John Young's Yard.

First Pillgwenlly Policeman appointed.

Pillgwenlly and the Commercial Wharves added to the Borough.

1837

Embankment at Town Dock (under construction) collapsed because of wet weather. Happened at night otherwise construction workers would have been killed.

Many new ships launched at the Yards of Pillgwenlly.

Sarah Sutton committed for trial for aiding in the removal and escape of John Hill from the custody of Sheriff's Officer.

Sergeant Redman dismissed from Head of Police in the Borough and replaced by Sgt Hopkins of Bristol.

Rees Rees becomes Head of Pillgwenlly Police—salary 12 shilling per week (60p).

Tredegar Arms Hotel, Church Street, up for auction.

1838

Money raised by selling shares to further finance the new Dock.

Canal frozen over and all traffic stopped.

More new ships launched from Pillgwenlly Shipbuilding Yards.

The poor of Pillgwenlly given bread, potatoes and herrings by the generosity of Sir Charles Morgan, Samuel Homfray, J F Hanson and a Mr Vaughan.

James Williams, a pilot, found dead beside the Tram Road in George Street.

Samuel Williams charged with committing a rape on the person of Ann Perrin servant to Mr Venn of Pillgwenlly.

Pillgwenlly Sunday Schools take part in Whitsuntide March through the town.

Regetta and boat race held on the river.

Exports from wharves increase.

Boiler bursts on steam locomotive "St David" near Court-y-Bella.

1839

Watch Committee put up street name identification plates. House numbering to follow.

Recently widowed pregnant mother named Feeham with three small children, falls down ballast bank in treacherous conditions near Town Dock and is killed.

Request to Parliament for loan to help finish the construction of the new Town Dock.

Burglary of premises of Harper (Grocers).

Service held on the barque "The Bethel" before setting sail for Philadelphia. Capt Marshall the Master of the ship takes part in prayers.

More new ships launched.

Mr Homfray agrees to use his Old Corn Mill as a Barracks for Troops.

John Davis and Richard Prosser apprehended in Temple Street in connection with Chartist Riots.

Dispensary opened in Llanarth Street. Forerunner to the Royal Gwent Hospital.

1840

Soldier of the 45 Regiment under arrest in Barracks severely injured in trying to attempt escape.

Extensive damage at Clarke's Pottery caused by fire.

Bathing in the nude in the Canal and River Usk criticised by the Mayor.

Wm Edwards, an apprentice, killed aboard the schooner "Pillgwenlly".

Many accidents and drownings in Pillgwenlly caused by the treacherous conditions.

Mr Hopkins, late landlord of the Salutation Hotel, dies suddenly while fishing.

Newport Steam Tug Company launched.

Residents complain about postage rates in Pillgwenlly which are higher than in other parts of Borough.

Work on construction of new Town Dock continues despite set backs.

Thos Prothero offers £100 reward for information leading to conviction of person who set fire to his hay rick at Court-y-Bella Farm.

Water obtained from wells at this time or bought from street hawkers.

1841—January

Young widow named Donohu "picking" coal from Tram Road, run over by a tram and has leg severed.

Destitution caused by stoppage of work on New Town Dock. Families almost starving. Trying to exist on boiled turnips and bread.

March

Complaints of filthy and dangerous condition of pavements near George Street. Very broken, and sunk with pools of water ankle deep.

New Post Office for Pillgwenlly agreed as a result of application by R J Blewitt, Esq, MP to the Postmaster General.

April

Work resumes on New Town Dock. Good progress made. Nearly 300 men employed.

May

Man seriously injured by gunshot wounds near Pillgwenlly Barracks. Shot accidently in firing practice by the Rifle Brigade.

August

Woman named Mary Stone who kept a Lodging House near the New Town Dock hangs herself. Said to have been owed much money by men working on the construction of the Docks.

September

Boy aged 13 working on New Docks run over by tram. Legs shattered. Died later in Devonshire House, Dock Parade.

1842—January

Soup Kitchens set up to alleviate hunger and misery.

Alarming fever which had been rampant amongst the poor begins to subside.

March

Police Station suggested for Pillgwenlly in view of increasing population and property.

April

William Pennimore (later to be stationed in Pillgwenlly) appointed to the Police.

July

Much vandalism done to houses and gardens in George Street.

PC No 4 (Henry Hayward) reported to the Watch Committee for neglecting part of his beat at Jacks Pill and Commercial Wharf between 2.00 am and 5.00 am. Fined ten shillings and severely reprimanded.

September

Pill women in Court after fighting about their straying pigs. Nuisance caused by filth created by pigs referred to by Magistrates.

October

New Town Dock opened.

Magistrates refuse to renew the licence of "The Old Red Cow"—a notorious pub in Canal Parade.

1843—February

John Williams, son of a corporal bugler of the 73rd Regiment stationed at Pillgwenlly seriously injured by a tram in the Court-y-bella area. Many other accidents involving trams.

June

16th Anniversary Services of the Mariners' Chapel, Jacks Pill held; presided over by the Mayor, R Mullock Esq.

Attention called to the wretched state of the roads approaching the Barracks. Mill Parade residents find difficulty in getting to hear the band concerts performed on Sundays by the 73rd Regiment.

August

Foundation stone of Welsh Baptist Chapel, Commercial Road (Y Demyl) laid by W Williams, Timber Merchant.

October

Wharf belonging to Rosser Thomas collapses. One man killed, others injured.

December

"The Astrea" sinks in New Dock.

Sir Charles Morgan's Cattle Show at Court-y-bella a great success.

1844—January

Ann Parry of Canal Parade dies after reaching her 105th birthday. Had her last tooth extracted when over 100. *Monmouthshire Merlin* quotes "This ancient woman expired like the last glimmer of a wasted lamp—without pain or struggle and full of the certain hope of a joyful hereafter."

February

Tram road accidents still common, especially among children.

Necessity of new Cattle Market urged to replace the one in the Town Centre at High Street.

March

Serious accident to apprentice aboard "The Clytha" in New Docks.

May

100 ton Schooner launched from Yard of Morgan Davies.

June

New Town Docks busy.

Jenkin Morgan former Dairyman of Pillgwenlly who was arrested at the time of the Chartist Riots released from Penitentiary in a bad state of health.

Welsh Baptist Temple, Commercial Road (Y Demyl) opened for worship. Services preached in English and Welsh by Rev Thomas Morris (Pastor) and Rev H Poole (Abergavenny). Building packed. Collection liberal.

September

"William Melville" launched from Yard of Cook and Young.

New Cattle Market opened at Tredegar Street to relieve nuisances caused in Town Centre by straying cattle, filth, smells and congestion.

Annual Newport Fair held at the New Cattle Market for the first time.

November

Young girl (aged two) left at home by parents at Custom Boat House, Pillgwenlly, severely burnt.

1845—January

First horse omnibus to run between Town and Pillgwenlly. Described in the Press as "having a pleasing appearance and being so long a desideration (a thing to be desired); substantial and comfortable drawn by good nags and provided with careful attendants."

May

Fire aboard "The Diamond" in new Docks. Horse drawn fire engine arrived too late. Ship scuttled to extinguish fire.

75th Regiment vacate Barracks at Pill and march through town to new Barracks at Malpas.

July

Margaret Parry (12) of High Street (now St Michael Street) walking along Tram Road near the Waterloo Turnpike Gate severely burnt by glowing embers from locomotive catching her dress alight.

August

Trade increases at New Town Docks.

September

Hayrick on fire at Mr Giddy's Farm. Fire put out by Police and others whilst attempt made to bring fire engine into use.

Commercial Road, the property of the Tredegar Company, in a disgraceful condition from the vast quantities of mud allowed to accumulate upon it and pools of water ankle deep.

New houses erected near Cattle Market.

One man drowned in Jacks Pill. Another saved from drowning by Dock Policeman Watts. Lack of public lighting blamed.

Temple Street opened.

Joseph Latch of Commercial Road (first Mayor of Newport) appointed Mayor for the second time.

1846—January

New Fire Engine tested at Canal Side—great success.

February

Pillgwenlly described as the dirtiest of all places where malaria may always be found. Particular reference to Court-y-bella Tram Road described as most filthy, poorly lit and dangerous. Deep holes and ravines between tram roads and not a solitary public light. Many accidents caused by dreadful conditions.

Streets described as "clothed with mud as with a garment."

March

Robbery and violence common.

April

Young lad named Morgan killed by a tram near the Courtybella Machine. Mother near confinement, father out of work and family destitute. Jury at Inquest give their fees to the family.

May

Captain of the Schooner "Mona's Isle" killed following accident aboard ship.

Young babies found abandoned; described as "child dropping". Others who had died found buried in ballast near Docks. Parents unable to afford burial.

Association Services held at Ebenezer Chapel. Chapel too small. Moved to New Cattle Market where services were held.

Cases of typhus fever in Pillgwenlly caused by bad ventilation, want of proper drainage together with accumulation of filth. Residents urged to ventilate and clean bedrooms, and clean yards using plenty of lime. Also asked to remove all heaps of foul matter and clean out cess pools.

June

Residents living around Cattle Market complain of noise from Fairs held there.

July

Straying horses cause accidents around the new Dock and Canal.

August

Several cases of cholera reported. Local press suggests two table spoons of the following mixture to be taken daily: six drachms prepared chalk; two drachms white sugar; two drachms gum arabic; thirty drops tincture of opium; thirty drops essence of ginger; $\frac{1}{2}$ oz tincture of cayenne; 7 oz of water.

Trade at New Town Dock good. Exports include rail iron and coal; imports include timber, apples, hay, flour, potatoes, oats, iron, coke, bricks, dates.

Newport August Fair held at the Cattle Market.

Irish peasants unwisely encouraged to leave their country to seek work in Newport. Many come on coal boats, with empty stomachs, only to find further poverty.

September

Tea at Independent Chapel, Temple Street. Proceeds for liquidation of debt.

October

Irish Seaman drowned at Town Dock.

December

Death of Sir Charles Morgan. Shops at Pillgwenlly close as a mark of respect.

Water obtained from rain and springs. Public spring at Pill derives its source from St Paul's Church.

1847—January

Eighteen year old seaman from "The Victoria" drowns in Docks after fall from ship.

February

New schoolroom for education of boys opened at rear of Wesleyan Methodist Church, Commercial Road, near Church Street. Cost £220 to build. To provide education for Wesleyan Methodists and others.

March

William Wilson of Pillgwenlly has finger removed by operation using "ethereal vapour producing insensibility". First time used in Newport. Patient said that he had no sense of pain during operation and expressed great surprise, on arousing from his happy slumber at seeing his finger on the floor.

April

William Kinlett killed in Potter Street after falling under a tram. Slipped whilst climbing embankment to get out of the way of travelling loaded trams.

Rat eats ear of live pig on premises of David Jones, Commercial Road.

Irish woman begging from door to door with corpse of infant in her arms.

Several cargoes of Irish people sent back to Ireland. Hundreds remain in starving condition.

May

Typhus still prevelant particularly amongst the destitute and starving Irish immigrants.

June

Newport Wool and Cattle Fair held at the Cattle Market.

October

Bread stolen from Mr Pell (Baker), Commercial Road.

Samuel King killed by tram in Commercial Road. Father killed at the same spot the previous year.

Boiler of new steam engine dragging carriages full of iron bursts in Commercial Road.

Two shilling pieces seen for the first time in Pillgwenlly.

Death of Thomas Davies who lived in Commercial Road near the Salutation Hotel. Fifteen years previously he made his own coffin and used it as his cupboard in which he kept his bread, cheese and other provisions. He also bought a piece of land at the burial ground of the Charles Street Baptist Church, at the head of which he put a stone inscribed with his name with blanks for his age and date of death. He gave instructions to his daughter that upon his death his body be "laid out" at the Baptist Temple, Pill (Commercial) Road and that he be carried "in his own coffin" to "his own grave". All these injunctions were fulfilled to the letter. Thomas was a Christian who read his Bible and prayed to his God daily. In more than one way he prepared for death.

Thomas Edwards, a hobbler, on board the barge "Eldon" killed. Father of five children. Inquest in Devonshire Arms, Dock Parade.

1848—January

Edward Batten, a pugilistic youth, and George Young, an old man, charged with fighting.

Consumption causes anxiety. Said to be caused by long confinement in close, ill-ventilated rooms.

Attack on Police by drunken sailors near the Britannia Beer House, Canal Side.

February

Cattle Market very busy.

Burglary at "Belle Vue" (now Belle Vue Park). Residence of Frederick Justice, Esq.

Newport and Pill Police Force consists of ten men, two Sergeants and one Inspector.

Danger caused by broken pavements mentioned in Council.

Steam packets trade between Newport and Liverpool for the first time.

March

Newport and Pillgwenlly Water Works Company start laying mains for "clear" water supply.

William Richards, a young man notorious for his fighting ability (called the "Pill Champion") charged with assaulting PC Kelly.

Lead stolen from roof of Ruperra Arms, Commercial Road.

April

Concern expressed that the prosperity at Pill would detract from the prosperity of the main part of Newport.

Violent thunderstorm causes flooding and damage to property.

Robbery at George Wilde's Pawnbroker's shop in Ruperra Street.

Ellen Bryant and Bridget Fitzgerald charged with stealing coal from the Town Dock.

James O'Brien, a young seaman, charged with leaving his vessel without permission.

Poor Irish immigrants brought into Newport by vessels unlicensed to carry passengers. Described as "unhappy beings sent across the sea with false hopes".

Pill mother and child severely injured by passing team of trams which ran over them.

Fine sloop "Burton" launched from Young and Cook's Yard.

Anniversary Services at Trinity Independent Chapel, Temple Street. Preachers Rev W H Lewis (Usk), Rev J Matthews (Neath), and Dr Isaac Harris (St Brides). Preaching in Welsh. Collections taken to clear debt on Chapel.

Houses built around the New Cattle Market. Some by "industrious mechanics"; some through the medium of Building Societies; and others by "capitalists".

Daily arrival of poor Irish immigrants, driven from their homes by eviction or famine. Reported to be trailing through the streets with nowhere to go in rags and barefooted. Children with bleeding feet crying in pain and misery.

Batty's Procession and Circus at the New Cattle Market attracts large crowds.

June

Sunday School Whitsuntide Festivities.

Fete and Gala at the Cattle Market.

July

Attendance at the Mariners' Church (first Church in Pill) declining.

Death of Mrs Pyne, highly respected Pill resident who had devoted most of her life to good works and charity.

Anniversary of Brotherhood of Oddfellows. Meet at Kings Arms Inn.

Body of infant found (in soap box and wrapped in linen) on bank of Pill near Tredegar Wharf. Infanticide suspected.

August

Newport August Fair held at the Cattle Market. Obstruction caused in Commercial Road by entrants "showing" horses in the street.

Hurricane causes damage to ships and property.

September

New Beer and Licensed Victuallers Act in force. Prohibits any house for the sale of beer being kept open later than 12.00 o'clock on a Saturday night and restricts opening on Sunday until divine worship has finished.

George Hall, an American seaman on board "The Marion" drowned in the Town Dock after he had been drinking. Police criticised for having no constables on duty at the Dock at the time of the tragedy.

Vessel in Rock Yard struck by lightning.

"The Princess Royal" Beer House, Commercial Road, for sale.

October

Municipal Elections. *West Ward* (inc Pill): H J Davies, Townsend and Webb elected. Garrett not elected. *East Ward*: Jenkins, Dowling and Davies elected, Williams not elected. Electorate: West Ward—268; East Ward—220.

Robbery from shop window of Mr Charles, clothier, Commercial Road. Clothes removed by cutting out portion of shop window.

November

Newport Annual Winter Fair held at the Cattle Market.

Tea Meeting at the Baptist Temple, Commercial Road well attended. Collection taken to liquidate debt on Chapel.

New Member of Council (Councillor W C Webb) displays a warm zeal for the interests of Pillgwenlly in Council meetings.

Ann Price and Susan Davies described as two "notorious disorder-lies" sent to prison for two months for their bad conduct in the street and for smashing windows.

December

Sir Charles Morgan's Cattle Show at the Cattle Market.

1849—January

Population of Pillgwenlly between seven and eight thousand.

First Police Station opened near "the well" in the Church Street area. Three Policemen to reside, but instructed to divide their time between Pillgwenlly and Newport until the general Force was increased.

Complaints of filth and muck near Canal.

New Wesleyan Chapel being built between Potter Street and Church Street on site of old Chapel built in 1832. Built in Norman style to accommodate seven/eight hundred people. The builders, Northcote and Cock, built the Chapel in about five months.

William Richards knocked overboard in New Docks. Body picked up by Dock Gates.

Robbery from schooner "Richard Hill" lying in The Pill at Pillgwenlly.

New hotel erected in Dock Parade opposite New Dock. Erected by Charles Parfitt, son of Dockmaster and landlord of the Devonshire House.

February

Alarming influx of Irish, mostly sickly and half starved.

Need for a Fire Brigade for the town suggested by Pillgwenlly residents.

March

Wesleyan Methodist Chapel between Potter Street and Church Street opened on Thursday 22 March. Speakers, Dr Beaumont of London; Rev Wm Arthur of Paris.

April

John James falls in water at Jacks Pill Bridge which was unlit. Fourth death at same spot.

May

More starving Irish immigrants arrive—some with the hand of death on their faces. Aged men and women, boys and girls clothed in rags and gaunt from famine come into an already overcrowded area.

June

Pillgwenlly Sunday Schools take part in Whitsuntide procession.

Cholera in Pillgwenlly not so bad as in other parts of Wales.

Pillgwenlly Wesleyan Day School's public examination highly gratified with proficiency in reading, writing, mental arithmetic, geography and grammar. Master—Mr William Morgan.

Foundation stone of Bible Christian Chapel, Commercial Road (near Alma Street), laid by Mr John Nance Kivell. Sermon preached in the open air by Rev Joseph Baker followed by tea in the New Cattle Market. Builders Northcote and Cock.

October

Seventh anniversary of opening of Town Dock. Many people visit to view ships called "floating castles". Many flags of different nations proudly displayed on masts of many ships.

November

Rev John Noall appointed Minister of Mariners' Church, Jacks Pill, referred to as a "Sabbath Haven for seafarers".

Baptist Temple, Commercial Road, hold Tea Party.

December

Bible Christian Chapel, Commercial Road, opened on Thursday 13 December with first Sunday Services on the 16th. Tea Party held in Cattle Market.

1850—January

Man falls down unprotected hole in pavement in Commercial Road near Albert Street and is severely injured.

PCs Bath and Long given rewards for capturing two sailors smuggling contraband goods.

Many deaths from cholera and other diseases cause shortage of burial ground.

David Wall charged with cruelty to a cat in Pillgwenlly field. Said to have thrown a sack over the cat and then set a dog on it. Each time the cat tried to escape Wall threw the sack over it and urged the dog to attack it. Wall appeared to see no harm in "the sport", but seemed to enjoy it.

Jame Mahoney (Est 1847) opens works in Portland Street.

February

Ship "Matilda" lying alongside a wharf in Pill on fire. No horses available to bring the fire engine to the fire, so Constables act as

horses. Engine too late in arriving, decided to put the fire out by
scuttling the ship. Repaired and set sail a few days later.

Ox escapes from slaughter house causing havoc in Pill. The infurated
beast subsequently killed by two musket balls.

PCs Miles and Hopkins censured and cautioned for pushing down
Mary Phillips outside the Pill Police Station when she broke her
arm.

March

The Salopian Wonder appears at the Cattle Market. The simple
entertainment consisted of him running a mile and picking up
forty stones placed a yard apart, depositing them in one heap;
walking a mile; rolling a coach wheel a mile; walking a mile back-
wards; picking up forty eggs placed a yard apart and placing them
in a basket.

Complaints about state of streets around the new Cattle Market.

Cargo of prime white French potatoes arrives at the Town Dock.

Town Dock busy. Talk of improving facilities to equal those at
Cardiff.

Large profits at Beer Houses cause concern. Suggested that the
popularity of these establishments described as "sinks of iniquity"
should be controlled by the Magistrates.

A huge brawny man named James Coles, a hobbler, charged with
assaulting PC Hopkins in one of the regular Sunday morning
Pillgwenlly riots.

April

Ship "Lady of the West" owned by W C Webb (new Pill Councillor)
suffers damage and loss of foremast. New foremast installed and
off again to sea as soon as a fair wind arrived.

George Pring, keeper of the "West of England" Beer House, fined
for allowing beer to be consumed at improper hours.

James Hatter who had been beating his wife, fined for assaulting
Ann Hallan who interfered with the beating.

Whitsuntide Festivities include Sunday School procession and hymn
singing, parties, and fireworks and a Fair at the Cattle Market.

May

Monmouthshire Baptists meet at the Cattle Market for Services.

Town Dock crowded with ships.

Catherine Kennedy, a prostitute charged with stealing a watch from
John Barber after "luring him to her den" at 5.00 am.

June

Charles Church, beer house keeper, charged with asaulting his wife.
PC Price finds wife in dreadful state and to "prove the case"
Church kicks his wife in the presence of the Constable.

Rev Noel preaches farewell sermon to the congregation at the
Mariners' Chapel prior to his departure as Pastor to a Church in
Northleach, Gloucestershire.

Depression in shipping trade caused by strike of colliers.

July

Beautiful cutter built by Mr Williams, boat builder, Town Dock, launched. Boat intended for Mr W Anstice, Pilot No 3.

John Roberts landlord of the "Three Mariners" public house in Lewis Street, dies whilst endeavouring to quell a disturbance created by sailors drinking at the pub.

Commodious and very tasteful railway carriage arrives from Birmingham for Mr Samuel Homfray, and is stationed at Tredegar Wharf.

New and improved Watchhouse "for the use of Government" erected on west bank of the Usk under the superintendence of Mr Samuel Homfray. Builder Mr Francis Coslett.

Two young Pill boys William Evans (12) and William Webb (9) drowned whilst bathing in the river Ebbw.

New buildings progressing so rapidly in Pill (Commercial) Road that Pill will shortly be connected to Newport.

August

New machine for loading coal to vessels erected at the Town Dock. Calculated to load 15 tons of coal in five minutes.

Cross Street Sunday battles amongst the quarrelsome inhabitants causes concern to the Police.

New dredge boat arrives at the Town Dock to clear mud from the docks.

Expelled Wesleyan Ministers hold conference in Newport. Mr Cole of Pillgwenlly expresses much pleasure at the increasing breadth and depth of the reform movement in Methodism.

Cherry Fair held at the Cattle Market.

"Well appointed" horse-drawn omnibus running to and from Pill. Started by enterprising townsman Charles Phillips.

Pillgwenlly Baptists' first Sunday School tea party held at the New Lodge Room, Kings Arms Inn. One boy repeats 783 verses of Scripture.

New Watchhouse on the west bank of the Usk rapidly approaching completion. Fine look-out from which "the watchman" may cast his eye far down the river and channel.

Mon Railway and Canal Company put gas lights in Temple Street, Portland Street and Church Street, through which their railways run.

Pill traders discuss early closing and decide to close their shops at 8.30 pm every evening except Saturdays.

Sir Charles Morgan and family attend Wombell's Menagerie at the new Cattle Market.

September

Rev Isaacs of the Branch Church, Pill, given a presentation as he leaves to move to Malpas.

Beer house keepers combine to form a subscription society to assist each other to pay heavy fines.

October

Complaints about lack of lighting on Pill (Commercial) Road.

December

Crowded audience attend the Baptist Temple, Commercial Road, to hear Mr Coleman, an expelled local Wesleyan preacher talk on "Popery of Methodism".

Council approve two additional Police in Pill (from 2 to 4), as one third of the Town's rates come from Pillgwenlly. PC Proverbs, a fine Policeman of Herculian proportions and another giant 6'6" tall, "from the hills" added to the Force.

New cutter built by Mr Williams at the Town Dock. Intended for Mr Gilmore, Pilot No 5. Probably the fastest boat in Newport and other ports.

Council concerned about disgraceful conditions in Pill.

Orphan School, Dolphin Street, for educating Orphans and very poor boys and girls, opens.

1851—January

Charles Wilkins falls off bridge at Jacks Pill and drowns. Had been drinking. Leaves wife and four young children.

Mr Cole, a Pillgwenlly Welseyan Dissenter, expelled from the official Wesleyan Group, starts an independent Church and Sunday School.

February

Overcrowding a great problem in Pillgwenlly. Seven room house occupied by fifty seven men, women and children huddled together on their beds of straw and shavings. One bed occupied by a sick man whilst around him lie, under the same dirty rug, five other human beings. Smell in house intolerable.

Ruperra Street and New Market Street contain pools of water deep enough for a child to drown.

Meeting held at the Wesleyan Chapel, Commercial Road, to discuss the erection of a building to be used by the New Mechanics Institute. Site fixed at the corner of Dock Street and Ruperra Street (Masonic HQ).

April

Commercial Road undergoes much needed repair.

Anniversary services at Wesleyan Chapel, Commercial Road.

May

Drownings continue at Town Dock and Canal caused by drunkenness, bad lighting and dreadful conditions.

Town Dock emptied of water to undergo repairs.

Ship constructed of iron built at Ukside Iron Foundry and launched successfully.

Trinity Independent Chapel, Temple Street, re-painted.

June

"Black Ball" raised at the Town Dock indicating that the Dock was full. Several ships advertise facilities for immigration.

Plymouth Brethren hold services at the Town Dock.

Cooke's Famous Circus held at the Cattle Market.

July

The Mayor (W C Webb Esq) presents a well-bound copy of the Scriptures to Pill Police Station and copies for prisoners to use in the cells.

Members of Tabernacle Church, Commercial Street, use Mariners' Church, Jacks Pill, whilst premises are renovated.

Houses erected around the Cattle Market and around Holy Trinity Church Site.

August

Shipping unable to get into Town Dock because of lack of space. Possible to walk across the Dock from ship to ship. Suggestions that Dock should be enlarged.

September

New Church being built at Potter Street (Holy Trinity) by John Hunt and Sons, to accommodate 600. To replace Trinity Independent Church, Temple Street.

October

Robberies at Town Dock common.

December

New two-horse-drawn street sweeping machine seen in Pillgwenlly for the first time.

"Christening" new Policemen common practice in Pillgwenlly (and Newport). PCs Jenkins and Gould victims of this practice on Christmas day. Officers beaten up by blackguards and ruffians.

1852—March

William Ashley of Bristol killed at Courtybella Station.

Young girl, Mary Sullivan pleads guilty to stealing water.

April

Election riots at Pill. Prospective MP W S Lindsay and friends attacked by Pill ruffians led by notorious bully known as "the Pill Pugilist".

May

William Gregory, cart porter, run over by his own horse and cart in Commercial Road near Ruperra Street and killed.

June

Andrew Nicholas, cook aboard "Ocean Star" murders Thomas Godfrey in Town Dock.

Holy Trinity Church, Potter Street, consecrated and opened.

July

Nuisances abound everywhere in Pill. Sluggish slime oozing out from half covered drains poisoning the air with foetid exhalations.

Tea Party held in Cattle Market by Wesleyan Reform Methodists.
Proceeds to build new Chapel in Pill. (Portland Street Methodist
Church.)
Band concert in Cattle Market by the 48th Regiment. Sir Charles
and Lady Morgan in attendance.

September

Ten "Dock Watchmen" appointed under Sergeant Long to guard
ships and property in the Town Dock.
Concert by 48th Regiment at Cattle Market cancelled because of
funeral of the late Mrs Homfray.

October

Foundation stone of new Wesleyan Reform Chapel, Portland Street,
laid.

December

Portland Street Chapel roofed.
Sir Charles Morgan's Annual Cattle Show at the Cattle Market.
Holy Trinity Church, Potter Street, supplied with gas.

1853—January

Council show pride in Town Dock by saying facilities far better than
those at Cardiff. Trade very busy and Docks nearly always full.

February

Pillgwenlly being rivalled by the expanding Baneswell which is
described as "a new Town".
Tea Party held at Trinity Church Hall to help pay for gas recently
installed at Holy Trinity Church, Potter Street. £16 raised.
Fire at premises of James Lewis, Draper, Commercial Road. Water
brought to Police by residents with buckets because of slow arrival
of horse drawn fire engine. One resident has pocket picked whilst
helping.

March

New Wesleyan Chapel opened in Portland Street.
Plasterers strike for higher wages.

April

Quarterly meeting of Wesleyan Reformers held at new Portland
Street Chapel. Since separation from main Wesleyans the Reform
Party in Newport has increased from 100 to 281 and possessed
two large Chapels.
Streets crowded with Irish immigrants.
Problems caused by ownerless dogs prowling the streets.
Rev T G Hodgson of Leamington succeeds Rev Woodruffe as Curate
of Holy Trinity Church.
Ships' flags at half mast in respect for Thomas Protheroe, Pill
businessman, recently died.
Several accidents, deaths and drownings at the Town Dock and the
Canal.

May

Whitsuntide processions and tea parties held by Sunday Schools.

Fifty children of the Sabbath School, Courtybella Street, under the guidance of Mr and Mrs Allen, enjoy a tea party in their school-room.

June

"Expelled" Wesleyan Minister preaches at Commercial Road and Portland Street Wesleyan Chapels.

August

Annual Newport Cherry Fair held at Cattle Market.

Water let out of Town Dock and Canal for clearing out mud, etc.

September

Complaints from Pillgwenlly residents about lack of street lighting. Gas company say that lighting will be supplied as soon as materials (pipes, etc) are available.

October

More new ships launched.

November

Labourers strike at Riverside Wharves.

Bill being prepared to go before Parliament to extend Town Dock.

December

Austrian Ship's Captain charged with threatening to murder Pilot William Parfitt.

1854—January

Part of Canal abandoned and later to be filled.

Pillgwenlly residents concerned about lack of repair and cleansing of streets. Thick mud on roads and pavements.

Congregation of Holy Trinity Church make presentation to Mr Watkins for the loan of his organ to the Church. New organ shortly to be installed.

March

Collections made at Trinity, Welsh Baptist and Wesleyan Churches for soldiers' families left at home (Crimean War).

Many petty thefts, some involving children, take place in Pillgwenlly.

Because of Crimean War Her Majesty proclaims a day of humiliation and prayer. Shops closed throughout Pillgwenlly and many people attend Church.

Many cases of drunkenness including those amongst women and young girls.

May

Embankment collapses at Jacks Pill.

Town Dock Extension Bill before Commons.

Harbour Police have different uniforms from Borough Police to distinguish the two Forces.

June

Pillgwenlly Sunday Schools join Newport Sunday Schools in March of Witness through the Town at Whitsuntide.

Newport Wool Fair held at Cattle Market.

Thomas Wood kills himself by hanging in Pill Lodging House.

July

New Custom House near Town Dock proposed.

August

Trinity School for Boys, Girls and Infants opens in Temple Street. Master—Mr Butt, Mistress—Miss Bush, Infants—Miss Newman.

Annual Newport Cherry Fair at the Cattle Market.

Large congregations at Holy Trinity Church, Potter Street. Gallery proposed to help accommodation problem.

September

Strike amongst stone masons working on Canal.

George Street residents burn effigy of Mrs H, who, after her husband had emigrated ,married a Mr W. She refused to go back to her husband after his return home.

November

New organ installed at Holy Trinity Church. Built by Mr Goddard of Dock Street.

Pillgwenlly and Newport become one. The following comment appeared in the *Monmouthshire Merlin* on 24 November 1854. "Until very lately these two places were far apart. The intermediate land in Commercial Road, however, is now so closely occupied by new and well built premises, that the old distinction exists no longer and the heretofore distant quarter at length merges its title in the general name of Newport."

December

Sir Charles Morgan's Annual Cattle Show at the Cattle Market.

Edward Sheeham, Master of Schooner "Cardine" found drowned.

Inquest at "Union Inn," Jacks Pill where Sheehan had been drinking the night he was drowned. (It was common at this time to hold Inquests in the local "hotels".)

1855—February

William Watkins, engine driver, killed by engine at Courtybella.

Ships sunk off Waterloo and Russell's Wharfs.

Tom, the Welsh rat catcher, catches 200 rats aboard the American ship "Mazatstan".

March

Extreme destitution amongst the poor of Pillgwenlly partially removed by help from the Churches and local firms.

Basic needs for family of man, wife and two children given as: Rent (2 small rooms) £1 10s; Wood 5/-; Water 3/6d; Bread (7 4lb (loaves) 10/6d; Meat (13lbs) 10/6d; Potatoes (10lbs) 5/10d; Tea

(2lbs) 2/-; Sugar (4lbs) 1/4d; Butter (1¼lbs) 4/6d; Candles and
Sundries 2/-. Total £3 14s 2d.

May

Henglers Circus at the Cattle Market.

Quarterly tea party at Dolphin Street Schoolroom given by Mr and
Mrs Allen for the children to whom they give educational and
religious instruction.

Town Dock very busy, "Black Ball", indicating that the Dock is full,
regularly seen.

The never ending tragedy of drownings in the Dock and Canal
continue.

June

Rev Hodgson leaves Holy Trinity Church for Pooly-bridge, Cumber-
land.

First Annual Meeting of Trinity School, Temple Street. School commenced in 1854 with 86 boys (now 126), 79 girls (now 113), 38
infants (now 125). No scholar admitted unless they attended a
Sunday School. Building also used for Pillgwenlly Bible Class,
Juvenile Temperance Society and Pillgwenlly Children's Missionary Association.

Sunday School Whitsuntide march through the Town. Pillgwenlly
schools take part.

Annual Wool Fair at the Cattle Market.

July

Residents still being killed and injured by dangerous conditions on
the roads mostly involving trams.

Rev John Jones, Minister of the Baptist Temple, Commercial Road,
gets a prize at the Welsh National Eisteddfod.

August

Trinity School, Temple Street, contemplate a new building for the
girls at Church Street (next to the Infants' School) so that the
Temple Street School can be used solely for boys.

Patrick Welsh bound over for threatening to shoot Enos Dix, a
hobbler, at Town Dock.

John Lewis and John Herbert sworn in before the bench as Dock
Policemen.

Newport Annual Cherry Fair held at the Cattle Market.

Laying of foundation stone to new Masonic Hall, Dock Street.
Procession from Town Hall to St Paul's Church for Service of
Worship and then to Dock Street via Commercial Road and
Ruperra Street. Architect for building: Mr Thomas of Great Dock
Street; Builder: Henry P Bolt. Cost £1,850.

Licensees of Beerhouses in Pillgwenlly fined for keeping open after
permitted hours.

September

Sermons preached on decks of ships in Town Dock.

"Mad" dogs prowling streets. Suggested they be shot as in Cardiff.

Horse drawn bus starts running between Town Dock and the Post
Office. Run by private enterprise.

Many cases of stealing, drunkenness and other crimes in Pillgwenlly.

Licensee of the "Crown and Anchor Inn", Canal Side, Castle Street,
fined for keeping "an improper house". 18-20 prostitutes alleged to
be on premises.

October

Electoral Roll shows 686 voters in East Ward and 623 in West Ward.

Jane Wiltshire and Emma Jones sent to prison with hard labour for
parading themselves as prostitutes and using bad language in
Church Street.

Tenders for new Trinity School in Church Street advertised.

Much drunkenness in Pillgwenlly.

Residents complain of high rates and poor services like lighting,
policing and street cleaning.

Jury return verdict of "Died by the visitation of God" on five year
old girl who died in school.

Foundation stone laid for new Girls' School in Church Street.

November

Man suffocated at Town Dock. Charcoal ignited in hold of ship to
kill rats and hatches put on, unaware that man still in hold.

December

Catherine Power fined for assaulting Mary Brown. Used bad language, tore off her cap and struck her in the face.

Docks full. Ships awaiting entry. Drowning still occurring.

1856—January

Pillgwenlly Workingmen's Institute opened at Trinity School, Temple
Street.

February

Henry Price, a haulier, killed at Carn Cethin Wharf.

March

Lectures given at Workingmen's Institute include : —

"The Working Man"—What is he?

"The Chemistry of Common Things"

"Encouragement to Effort".

April

Men charged with "working or causing men to work on the
Sabbath".

May

Rev John Jones, Minister of the Welsh Baptist Temple, Commercial
Road, presented with books for his faithful and zealous service.

June

Pillgwenlly Band of Hope excursion to Abergavenny.

July

Annual Meeting of Trinity Boys' and Girls' School at new Girls'
School, Church Street. Slight increase in numbers attending.

August

Work in progress on Town Dock Extension. Children playing in empty trams used for extension cause accidents.

September

New organ installed at Wesleyan Chapel, Commercial Road.

October

Soirée at Temple Street Schoolroom in aid of Pillgwenlly Workingmen's Institute.

November

Trinity School, Temple Street, advertise for a loan to keep school going.

Mr Perrin appointed organist at Holy Trinity Church.

Mr Druiff, a Jew, comes to the help of a family in great distress at 3 Portland Street. Supplies family with food to stop them from starving.

December

Shops close in Pillgwenlly just before Christmas to enable shop assistants to visit their friends.

Land slip on extension works to Town Dock.

Sarah Thomas of New Street charged with possible murder of one of her children.

Drownings and accidents in Pillgwenlly still causing concern.

Masonic Hall, Dock Street, opens.

1857—January

Rev John Jones, Minister of the Baptist Temple, Commercial Road, moves to Llangollen.

February

Anniversary Services of Wesleyan Methodist Society held at Wesleyan Chapel, Commercial Road.

Beer house offences, petty theft and drunkenness common.

Lecture "Electric Telegraph of England" given at Pillgwenlly Workingmen's Institute, Temple Street.

The "Moritz" of Riga, first Russian ship to enter Town Dock since declaration of war with Russia.

Man killed whilst demolishing a house on Canal Side. House being pulled down with rope attached to a horse.

March

Strike at Town Dock.

April

Concern that only half the children of Pillgwenlly attend Sunday School. Canvass to be made of whole area.

May

Extensions to Town Dock being carried out. First coal hoist in course of construction.

Sudden deaths "from natural causes" common. Health of inhabitants poor. Some "consumptive" patients.

June

Fires in Pillgwenlly often extinguished by residents before fire engine arrives.

Sunday School procession through the Town. Wesleyans have their own procession.

Mr Richard Poole of Sheffield preaches "revival sermons" in Portland Street Chapel and the Cattle Market.

Sunday School anniversaries at Bible Christian and Wesleyan Methodist Chapels, Commercial Road.

August

Quarterly meeting of the Orphan's Friend School, Dolphin Street. Christian organisation for the education of poor children (many orphans). Many received free education. Others paid one penny per week.

Concern over vice and depravity.

Pillgwenlly Lodge of the Odd Fellows opened at Tredegar Arms Inn.

Owners of unmuzzled dogs fined.

Preaching in the streets by the Mormons causes annoyance.

Newport Cherry Fair held at the Cattle Market.

September

Membership of Pillgwenlly Workingmen's Institute, Temple Street, reaches 150. Large Library well used by members.

Several drownings and serious accidents at Town Dock. Some caused by drunkenness, others by unruly horses.

1858—January

Pillgwenlly Band of Hope Drum and Fife band formed.

March

Anniversary of Pillgwenlly Temperance Society.

Anniversary of Portland Street Wesleyan Reform Chapel.

Second part of Town Dock opened.

April

Service held at Temple Street Schoolroom in aid of Holy Trinity Church Choir.

Inquest on George Lewis, lad of ten, at Kings Arms Inn. Fell whilst "picking" coal on top of a horse drawn tram. Horse jerked the poor lad off. Several trams passed over him.

May

Primitive Methodists hold District Meetings in Newport. Ten sermons preached in one day at the Cattle Market.

July

Newport and Pillgwenlly Band of Hope train excursion to Monmouth. Train load of 1,500 met by hundreds of friends. Town decorated in their honour.

September

Magistrates concerned about drunkenness in Pillgwenlly. Patrick Mead of Castle Street died following accident after being drunk.

October

Consecration of New Masonic Hall, Dock Street.

November

Young woman in High Street (now St Michael Street) deserts her child, "having no maternal feelings". Child later dies.

December

Bible Christian Church, Commercial Road, celebrate 9th Anniversary.

Pillgwenlly Choral Society give concert at Temple Street Schoolroom.

1859—January

Rev T Brookes Wrenford of Trinity Church given a presentation by his Bible Class. Only been in Pillgwenlly a few months but held in much affection by parishioners.

Trinity Church School hold concert and tea party to try to reduce debt on school.

February

Heavy westerly gale causes damage to shipping and the Dock at the Town Dock.

March

Lecture on "Astronomy" given to Pillgwenlly Young Men's Mutual Improvement Society.

Trade at the Town Dock improves after temporary slump. Much less unemployment in the area.

Pillgwenlly Police Station, Fire Engine House and Mortuary opened in Temple Street.

April

Ship launched at Willmott & Sons Yard, Jacks Pill.

Sir Charles Morgan becomes Lord Tredegar.

Special religious services for the working classes organised throughout Pillgwenlly.

May

Conditions in Lodging Houses better. Many free from contagious diseases.

June

Jacob Isaacs of Commercial Road robbed of gold and silver watches from his shop.

Mr John Willmott, shipbuilder, promises to build a war launch with a gun in the bow and six oars to defend the Port in case of attack!

Anniversary Services of Portland Street and nearby Wesleyan Chapel, Commercial Road.

Still many drownings and accidents at the Town Dock and the Wharfs.

July

Open air meetings held in the fields of Pillgwenlly by Wesleyan Methodists.

August

Pillgwenlly Workingmen's Institute "pic-nic" in fields at Pillgwenlly near the "Watchhouse".

September

New organ installed at Portland Street Chapel. Mayor contributes a sovereign towards cost.

Ann O'Neil, a prostitute, and Elizabeth Cooke a brothel keeper charged with stealing in Speedwill Street (near St Michael Street).

Holy Trinity Church short of money. Supply of gas cut off, and Church lit by candles.

October/December

Anniversary Services at Welsh Baptist Temple and Bible Christian Churches, Commercial Road.

1860—January

Voting at Pillgwenlly Police Station for Municipal Elections (West Ward). Mr Philips defeats Mr Murphy 220 votes to 146.

Seventeen adults baptised by total immersion at the Baptist Temple, Commercial Road.

Dead body of female baby found near the Salutation Hotel.

February

Concert at Temple Street Schoolroom under the guidance of Mr Perren, organist of Holy Trinity Church.

March

Fire at shop of Mr and Mrs Baker, Commercial Road, put out by neighbours before fire engine could arrive.

April

James Leger fined for allowing disorderly conduct in his Beer House in Church Street. Two men stripped and fighting in the back yard with Leger acting as "second" to one of them. Several prostitutes in the House which was in "great confusion".

John Kensey commits suicide by putting his head on tram rails and letting wheels of tram, drawn by three horses, run over it.

Orphans School, Dolphin Street, in financial difficulties. Since the school opened in 1850, 208 children had been educated, 111 orphans and 97 without fathers. Most given free education, but some paid a penny per week.

May

Holy Trinity Church appeal for financial help.

June

Annual Wool Fair at the Cattle Market.

July

Open air preaching at the Cattle Market delivered by a Mr Leach.

September

Man, depressed by unemployment, attempts suicide by cutting his throat in house in George Street.

Much drunkenness.

June

Band of Hope excursion to Abergavenny. Procession leaves Cattle Market and proceeds through Town to the station accompanied by their fife and drum bands.

Trinity Boys' School, Temple Street, closes because of lack of money. Girls' school in Church Street also likely to close.

October

Financial position of Holy Trinity Church improves.

November

Town Dock busy.

December

Pillgwenlly Workingmen's Club announces closure. Library of 300 volumes and furniture, etc, auctioned by Graham and Co.

Drownings and accidents (some causing death) common. Drunkenness, bad conditions and carelessness main causes.

1861—January

Recently dissolved Workingmen's Institute, Temple Street, determined to form another Society under the designation of Pillgwenlly Reading Room.

Jane Curtis, a prostitute, fined two shilling and six pence or 14 days imprisonment for being drunk and disorderly in Commercial Road. Man named Vegoe fined five shillings or 14 days imprisonment for attempting to "rescue" her from the Police.

Not so many children attending the Orphans School, Dolphin Street, as parents of paying students could not even afford to pay the penny per week because of trade depression.

February

Because of trade depression many people in Pillgwenlly unable to pay their rates.

March

Few ships in Town Docks.

April

Irish woman named Hannah Coghlan killed whilst stealing coal at the Town Dock.

May

Population of Newport at this time 24,164 (1,000 more females than males), nearly 4,000 inhabited houses in Newport.

John Thomas charged with keeping an unmuzzled dog.

Three prostitutes from Friars Field, named King, Howells and Williams, charged with using obscene language in Canal Parade.

Large congregations at Anniversary Services at Wesleyan Chapel, Commercial Road.

Mr Rogers' Pottery in Baldwin Street converted to a dwellinghouse.

Six hundred inhabitants of Pillgwenlly sign a petition and present it to Mr Samuel Homfray asking him to provide "a general market" in Commercial Road. Working people in the area not paid their wages until late on Saturday night and find difficulty in getting to Town to buy their groceries.

Annual Whitsuntide March, Pillgwenlly Sunday Schools take part.

Annual Wool Fair at the Cattle Market.

July

Miss Jollow, a lady from Devon, preaches at Bible Christian and Welsh Temple Chapels, Commercial Road.

Orphan School, Dolphin Street, in better financial condition. Fifty-six children attend daily.

August

Wesleyan Theological Class present Rev S P Havard with a silver salver as a token of their esteem.

Meeting at Holy Trinity Church to discuss the reopening of the day schools in Temple Street and Church Street.

Rev Edwards of Llanelly comes to Pillgwenlly to start a work for the English Baptists. Room at No 1 Portland Street given to him free of charge for one year to hold services by Mr J Northcote, another Christian. (This was the beginning of Commercial Road Baptist Church which opened in 1863 and closed a hundred years later.)

November

Serious accident at the junction of Portland Street and Commercial Road involving two horse drawn vehicles.

Improved trade at the Town Dock.

Several sudden deaths of babies.

Vessel "George Rutstone" launched from Willmott's Yard.

Pawnbroking increases to a great extent.

Holy Trinity Church makes approaches for a separate Ecclesiastical District for Pillgwenlly.

December

Mr Thomas Garratt, Master of the Wesleyan Voluntary School, Commercial Road, issues an encouraging report of his "Ragged" School.

Many burglaries in Pillgwenlly. Residents warned not to leave premises unattended.

Still many accidents caused by bad conditions and a number of drownings in the Town Dock, the wharfs and the canal.

1862—January

Financial position of Orphan Day School, Dolphin Street, better. Lord Tredegar donates a sovereign.

Commercial Road Baptist Sunday School started in Portland Street.

February

Trade good at Town Dock.

March

William Dallimore, a fatherless lad charged with stealing cakes from the Tredegar Inn Eating House. Ordered to be detained one day and to be whipped by Sergeant Bath.

Trinity National Schools in Temple Street and Church Street renovated at a cost of £130 and re-opened. Mr Roach from Highbury College appointed Master. Miss Dobbin, from Brighton Training College appointed Mistress. Miss Newman in charge of Infants. Also three pupil teachers. Pupils—90 girls, 80 infants, 70 boys. More money needed to clear debts of renovation.

April

Woman aged 31 of Company's Row died in childbirth. Baby alive and well.

Large congregations at Anniversary Services at Wesleyan Chapel, Commercial Road.

May

Edward Pitman (age 11) of Courtybella Street, meets with deplorable accident whilst working at Mr James' Pottery Works. Little chance of lad recovering.

June

Pillgwenlly Band of Hope (Juvenile Teetotallers) go to Caerphilly for Annual Excursion accompanied by their drum and fife band.

William Miller, keeper of the "Sailors Return" beer house, Commercial Road, fined £5 for keeping a disreputable house. Proceedings carried on at beer houses described as disgraceful—music constantly played, and girls who conduct themselves indecently turned out half a dozen at a time.

July

Anniversary Services of Newport Seamen's Mission held at the Mariners' Church near Jacks Pill. During the year 2,500 vessels visited; 6,000 tracts distributed; 150 sermons preached; 100 prayer meetings held.

Rev S Fox, Incumbent of Holy Trinity Church, given a presentation at Temple Street Schoolroom, for loyal services.

Population of Pillgwenlly about 6,000.

Holy Trinity Church licsensed for the solemnisation of marriages for the first time.

Coal shipped from Town Dock in 1861, 617,227 tons compared with 629,200 tons in 1860.

Abandoned baby found dead near Frederick Street.

Negotiations begin to make Holy Trinity Church, Potter Street, completely separate from St Paul's Church, Commercial Street.

Seamen's Mission opens in Williams Street. Accommodation for 200. Rev Isaac White, Chaplain. Services Tuesday, Thursday, Friday and Saturday evening.

August

Ann Morgan of Canal Side, commits suicide by drowning.

First marriage takes place at Holy Trinity Church between Mr P Sindgren and Miss Baker both from the ship "Salem" lying in the Dry Dock.

September

Thirteen year old Mary Ann Dick burnt to death near Watchhouse Parade whilst lighting a candle.

Branch of Wesleyan Church, Commercial Road, hold Tea Meeting near the Watchhouse.

November

Newport and Pillgwenlly Band of Hope hold Eisteddfod at the Town Hall.

December

Anniversary Services at the Bible Christian Church, Commercial Road.

Many drownings and accidents at the Town Dock and in the area generally.

1863—January

Wife of the Keeper of the "Mahoney Bar" beer house, High Street (now St Michael Street), runs away with one of the lodgers.

February

Mr Albert Hicks of Ruperra Street, an agent for a large Irish pig dealer, fined for having in his possession diseased pigs.

Tea at Portland Street Methodist Free Church to pay farewell tribute to Miss Pritchard, organist.

Average weekly attendance at Trinity Schools, Temple Street and Church Street: boys 120, girls 72, infants 110. Balance in hand £9 10s 9d.

April

Roy Evan Thomas of Charles Street Baptist Church, becomes Minister of Commercial Road Baptist Church.

May

New Shipbuilding Company headed by Crawshaw Bailey, Esq, proposed for Pillgwenlly.

Owners of unmuzzled dogs subject to fine of forty shillings.

June

Early closing of shops on Thursdays started.

Mary Vines, Keeper of the "Royal Oak" beer house in Ruperra Street, fined for keeping open after hours.

Open air preaching causes nuisance at Cardiff Road outside the "Salutation Inn' near "The Pump".

Annual Wool Fair held at the Cattle Market.

July

Services held in Commercial Street Baptist Church to commemorate the laying of memorial stones at the New Baptist Chapel, Pillgwenlly (Commercial Road Baptist Church). Memorial stones laid by G W Jones, Esq, Mayor. Tea and public meeting held in the Cattle Market.

August

George Gammon, licensee of the "Salutation Inn', Cardiff Road, fined for keeping a disorderly house. Twelve prostitutes alleged to have been in the premises.

Trade at the Town Docks still good.

September

Mary Ann Grumbledon, Keeper of the "Green Fields of America" beer house, Caroline Street, fined for supplying beer to nearby brothel at 2.30 am.

Anniversary services at Wesleyan Chapel, Commercial Road, well attended.

Arrangements to make Pillgwenlly a separate Ecclesiastical District reaching conclusion.

October

Disturbances at brothels in Pillgwenlly.

November

English Baptist Chapel, Pillgwenlly, opened (Commercial Road Baptist Church).

December

Thomas Kennedy and Thomas Sullivan fined for being drunk and disorderly in Castle Street. Challenged to fight any person who felt disposed.

Still many drownings in Town Dock, and riverside wrafs.

1864—January

Increase to Dock and Dry Dock accommodation discussed.

Eliza Thomas fined ten shillings or fourteen days' imprisonment for being a disorderly prostitute and assaulting the wife of the licensee of the "Salutation Inn".

February

Fourteenth Anniversary of Orphan Day School, Dolphin Street. School still struggling to remain open. Mr Allen, the Master, had laboured for fourteen years without any salary.

Mechanics Institute suggested for Pillgwenlly Street premises (Masonic Hall) too far away.

James Saunders charged with deserting his ship "Minerva" in Town Dock.

March

Newport Ragged Schools propose new buildings opposite the Drill Hall, Dock Street.

More drownings (including children) and fatal accidents (particularly to seamen) at the Town Dock.

April

Pillgwenlly Reading Room opened. Rev Samuel Fox (Incumbent of Holy Trinity Church) President.

Child poisoned by drinking liquid used in photography at Isaac Lyons' photographic shop, Commercial Road.

Holy Trinity Church becomes separate from St Paul's Church, Commercial Street, and Pillgwenlly becomes an independent ecclesiastical area.

June

Beer houses in Pillgwenlly criticised. Many open after hours and used for prostitution. "The Crown" beer house, Commercial Road, said to be the worst in Newport.

July

Trade brisk at Town Dock.

Sunday School Anniversary Services at Wesleyan Chapel, Commercial Road, well attended.

August

Annual excursion of the Newport Roman Catholic Association for the Suppression of Drunkenness. Procession leaves Cattle Market, and marches through Town to the Station. Mayor and several priests lead procession.

Sermons preached at Wesleyan Chapel, Commercial Road, in aid of recently established branch Sunday School at Watchhouse Parade.

Annual Cherry Fair at the Cattle Market.

September

New Docks for Newport suggested on land known as "the Hundred Acres" on the western side of the River Usk (now Alexandra Dock).

New stained glass window costing 100 guineas placed in Holy Trinity Church.

October

Ann White, a little girl, ordered to be detained for one day for stealing coal which she exchanged for apples at a Pillgwenlly Greengrocer's Shop.

Seamen's Home suggested.

November

Abandoned baby found in East Market Street.

Wesleyan Methodist Ragged School opened in Dock Street (opposite Drill Hall).

"Penny Readings" given at Temple Street Schoolroom (alternating weekly with similar "Readings" given at the Temperance Hall, Dock Street). ("Penny Readings" consisted of readings of poetry and prose with solos, instrumental solos, etc.)

1865—January

New Wesleyan Day School opened at the rear of Wesleyan Chapel, Commercial Road. Master—Henry Taylor of the National Training College, Westminster (reputed to be one of the earliest socialists). Terms six pence per week (six shillings per quarter)—First Class. Four pence per week (four shillings per quarter—Second

Class. Two pence per week (two shillings per quarter)—Third
Class.

Alexandra Docks Bill passing through the Commons.

February

Methodist Mission Services at Wesleyan Chapel, Commercial Road.

March

Ellen Jones, a brothel keeper, and Lucy Ann Powell, a prostitute,
fined for being drunk and disorderly in Canal Parade.

Serious fire at Williams' Pottery Works.

May

Twelfth Anniversary Services at Portland Street Methodist Free
Church.

June

New Alexandra Theatre opened in Lewis Street.

July

Alexandra Docks Bill passed by Parliament.

First public examination at Wesley Day School: Scholars 295;
accommodation for 350.

August

Residents fined for keeping pigs so as to be a nuisance. Pigs allowed
to stray into Trinity Churchyard.

September

Level crossing keeper cut to pieces by tram in Commercial Road.
Accident caused by runaway horse.

October

C H Spurgeon, famous London Preacher, preaches at the Cattle
Market. Admission by ticket only, costing one shilling. Crowds of
between ten and twelve thousand attend.

Bible Christian Church, Commercial Road, celebrated fifty years
since their denomination started.

November

Contract for construction of Alexandra Dock signed.

First Government Examination of Wesleyan Day School. 213
scholars present. 99% passed.

Drownings persist at Town Dock.

"Penny Entertainment" given at the Seamen's Bethel, Williams Street.

1866—January

Tea and concert given for the aged poor of Pillgwenlly at Seamen's
Bethel, Williams Street.

Quick turn-around of ships at Town Dock praised.

Accidents and drownings continue at the Town Dock.

February

Seamen sent to prison with hard labour for refusing to go to sea in
the British ships "Zetus" and "Charles Ward". Seamen say ships
not seaworthy.

Pillgwenlly children attend Annual Treat for Ragged Schools. After
tea and cakes the children given clothing and, before going home,
an orange, a copy of "The Band of Hope" and a *bon-bon*.

March

Town Dock filled with shipping.

Meeting of Alexandra Dock Company to discuss commencement
of work at new Docks.

Much drunkenness and crime in Pillgwenlly.

April

All shipping cleared from Town Dock in order that it might be
cleansed.

May

Lady Tredegar cuts first sod at Alexandra Docks.

Roaming dogs cause nuisance. Residents ask why they are not muzz-
led, tied up or shot.

June

Pillgwenlly Sunday Schools join in Whitsuntide festivities. Many have
Whitsun Fields. Procession through the town not held because
organisers say that numbers have come to such a proportion as to
be unmanageable.

July

Man named Mansfield sent for trial for stabbing incident at Music
Shop in Commercial Road, kept by a Mr Warnken. Shop fre-
quented by seamen and prostitutes.

William Bartlett fined five shillings for cruelly ill treating a horse
and working it in a Pillgwenlly Pottery, with two large wounds
the size of five shilling pieces, on its shoulders.

Sunday School Anniversary Services of Wesleyan Chapel, Commercial Road.

September

Deaths from cholera in Pillgwenlly. Mr Morgan and Mr Howard,
Chemists in the area instructed to give free medicine to anyone
suffering from diarrhoea. Building for the reception of cholera
patients erected on "the ballast bank".

Uskside Works, Church Street, taken over by new Company and
called "The Uskside Company".

Young son of Rev Isaac White, recently retired Chaplain of Seamen's Mission, Williams Street, drowned in pond at Williams'
Pottery.

October

Favourable change in the wind brings many ships to the Town
Dock.

Alma Street Baptist Church (now Emmanuel Evangelical Church)
founded in a sail loft in Canal Parade.

Old woman named Catherine Power missing from her home. Last
seen drunk near one of the wharfs. Believed drowned.

November

Methodist Circuit tea held at Portland Street Chapel. Members in congregation increasing.

December

Anniversary Services at the Bible Christian Chapel, Commercial Road, attended by the Mayor (Wm Graham, Junior).

1867—January

"Pillgwenlly Magazine" launched in Pill by Holy Trinity Church, price 1d.

February

Martha Jones, of Bolt Street, committed to two months' hard labour for stealing a pair of stays and a crinoline.

Seven year old son of Mr Howard, Pillgwenlly Chemist, drowned in the River Ebbw.

March

Penny Readings held at Trinity Boys' School, Temple Street.

Distress among Dock labourers. Lack of shipping in Town Dock through prevailing easterly wind preventing shipping from entering the Port with consequent lack of work. Some families in distress from hunger.

Pill Wesleyan Sunday Schools make presentation to Mr W F Stevens who had been a fellow worker for fourteen years (six years as Superintendet of Watchhouse Parade Branch Sunday School).

April

Concern expressed at continued closure of Cattle Market to cattle because of rinderpest.

Juvenile Choir of Pill Baptist Church (200 strong) gives concert at the Town Hall.

Proposed closure of Pillgwenlly Reading Room which has been in existence for over twenty five years. Meeting arranged at Temple Street Schoolroom to consider survival.

Meeting of Alexandra Dock Company. Rumoured that work on Alexandra Dock to commence soon.

May

Concert held to inaugurate the opening of the Pillgwenlly Institute (Reading Room).

Many Pillgwenlly children take part in Whitsuntide procession and enjoy a time at the Whitsun Fields.

June

Annual Wool Fair at the Cattle Market.

July

Wesleyan Day School, Commercial Road, congratulated by the Mayor (Wm Graham, Jnr) on its high standard.

Annual Sermon on behalf of the Newport Seamen's Mission preached at the Mariners' Church. Mariners' Home suggested for Newport.

New Drill Hall, Dock Street, near George Street (opposite the
Custom House) opened.
August
Newport Regatta held at Dock Head.
September
Circus held in building in Lewis Street under the management of
Mr W Wheal.
Boy preacher, Probert, preaches at the English Baptist Church
(Commercial Road Baptist Church).
First Penny Readings at the Pillgwenlly Institute at Temple Street
Schoolroom, presided over by the Mayor.
October
Cattle Market re-opened to cattle.
November
Newport Annual Fair at the Cattle Market.
Much crime in Pillgwenlly.
Drownings and accidents in the area still continue.
December
Subscription list for building of the Alexandra Dock set up. Much
money subscribed.
Christmas Treat given to Wesleyan Methodist Sunday Ragged
Schools at the School Room, Dock Street. Scholars and parents
attend.

1868—January
Three houses in Dolphin Street sold for £292 10s.
Police campaign against Brothel Keepers a success. Many Brothels
vacated.
Plans for houses in Alma Street, Raglan Street and Williams Street
approved by the Council.
Complimentary concert to Miss Nichols (Organist) at Portland Street
Methodist Free Church. Items rendered by Newport Vocal Union.
February
Dr W T C Pratt of Commercial Road appointed Medical Inspector
of Seamen.
First of new series of Penny readings under the patronage of the
Pillgwenlly Institute held at Temple Street Schoolroom.
Extra galleries erected in Wesleyan Church, Commercial Road to
accommodate growing congregations.
April
Eisteddfod held at Ebenezer Welsh Presbyterian Church, Commercial
Road.
Serious case of stabbing at the Town Dock.
Many drownings and accidents at the Town Dock.
May
Extension of Borough Boundary proposed to include new Alexandra
Dock.

June

Contractors (Griffiths & Thomas) start work on construction of Alexandra Dock. Several hundred men employed.

Charles Pearce (16) and William Davies (14) commended for saving two brothers named Gregory (12 and 14) from drowning in Brickyard Ponds.

July

Committee set up to provide a Seamen's Home in Pill.

Mr Taylor, Master of Pillgwenlly Day School, congratulated on the high standard of his pupils. Average attendance 273 pupils.

August

First fatal accident at Alexandra Dock. Boy named Thomas Pepperall killed by horse-drawn wagon. (Both steam and horse power being used on Dock construction.)

September

Seamen's Home opened in Dock Street.

November

PC John Maule, Harbour Police, drowned near Dock Head.

December

Hundred members of Wesleyan Ragged Schools enjoy a Christmas Treat.

1869—February

About 150 navvies employed on construction of Alexandra Dock go on strike, refusing to accept seventeen shillings per week. Contractor re-advertises their jobs immediately.

April

Child, age two, burnt to death in Canal Parade.

May

Mary Ann Attwell, caretaker of the English Baptist Chapel (Commercial Road Baptist Church) commits suicide by drowning in Town Dock. Paid four shilling per week by Church.

Appeal to the public to supply second hand clothing (especially boots) to Ragged Schools.

Whit Monday Fete at the Cattle Market.

Mary Ann Wallet charged with deserting her child. Leaves it on doorstep of 15 Williams Street.

Ann Tanner, 19 year old girl from York, who had given herself up to an immoral life, found guilty of murdering her new born baby. She delivered the child herself and cut its throat with a knife in the "British Flag" Beerhouse in Castle Street where she resided.

Sunday School Whitsuntide activities curtailed by bad weather.

June

Mr Bryant, Master of Trinity Church School, Temple Street, holds Annual Tea Meeting for scholars.

Annual Wool Fair at the Cattle Market.

July

"Foundation Stone" laid at Alexandra Dock.

Fire at Town Dock disturbs crowd watching Newport Regatta.

Serious accidents to men working on construction of Alexandra Dock.

August

Annual Cattle Fair at the Cattle Market.

Two children belonging to a navvy working at the Alexandra Dock abandoned. Taken care of by a Mr and Mrs Tasker.

Escaped bullock attacks children in Commercial Road. Child named Leary severely injured.

Town Dock trade improves and recovers from recent stagnation.

Lord Tredegar inspects progress at Alexandra Dock.

September

Rev T Rees leaves Holy Trinity Church. Succeeded by Rev Jones.

October

Council approve erection of houses in Lewis, Alma and Castle Streets.

November

The steamer "Ybarra" laden with 700 tons of iron ore sinks in Town Dock. Later salvaged.

Thought being given to second river crossing—eventually resulting in the opening of the Transporter Bridge in 1906.

Annual Stock Fair at the Cattle Market.

Drownings at Town Dock include children bathing and playing in small boats.

Much vice, crime, drunkenness, etc. in Pillgwenlly.

1870—January

John Legge sentenced to six months' imprisonment for refusing to go to sea.

Two hundred and fifty children from the Ragged Schools enjoy their annual free meal at the Ragged School, Dock Street.

Work suspended on construction of Alexandra Dock caused by possible bankcruptcy of Contractors. Many men out of work, and destitution in the area. Soup kitchens set up and coal distributed.

Bazaar held at Trinity Temple Street Schoolroom in aid of funds for the school. £30 raised.

February

Mary Ann Davies aged 43 dies as a result of burns. Deceased had no bed and slept on the floor in front of the fire with her husband.

March

Erection of houses in Lewis Street and Alma Street approved by the Council.

April

The "Kings Arms" public house burgled by the notorious burglar Daniel Shean.

Keepers of public houses and beer houses fined for keeping illegal hours and for allowing prostitutes on premises.

May

Foundation stone for Synagogue at the junction of Lewis Street and Francis Street laid by Mr Abraham Isaacs. Bottle placed underneath the stone containing a copy of the *Jewish Record,* new coins of the realm and local papers. Builder, J. W. Black. Architect, B Lawrence. Cost £800.

Concern expressed about the evil of drunkenness, particularly on Sundays. Between ten and fifteen cases per day before the Courts. Incidents of men lying helplessly drunk in the streets, often surrounded by hundreds of amused children on their way to Sunday School.

Photographs of work at the Alexandra Dock praised.

"Lunatic" attacks mason working on Holy Trinity Church.

Work on Alexandra Dock continues. Two hundred more men needed. Malicious damage caused to equipment at the Docks by unknown vandals.

June

Seamen's Bethel, Williams Street, re-opened after repairs, alterations and cleaning. Mariners' Seamen's Church at Jacks Pill now only used on Sundays for the benefit of the Scandinavian seamen.

Three thousand Sunday School children parade through the Town at Whitsuntide. Many go to Whitsun Fields in the afternoon.

House fitted out as a Chapel in High Street (now St Michael Street) for St Michael's RC Church.

New pilot boat "Fleetwing" launched at Dock Head.

Police still responsible for fire fighting.

Temperature in Pillgwenlly 118°F.

Annual Wool Sale at the Cattle Market.

July

Many "irregularities" at beer houses. "British Flat" in Castle Street not licensed.

Wesleyan Day School, Commercial Road (Master: Henry Taylor), highly commended by Her Majesty's Inspector of Schools. Average attendance 284.

August

Annual Cattle Fair held at the Cattle Market.

Trinity Day Schools, Temple Street, and Church (Master: Mr H Joliffe), get increase in Government grants because of good progress.

September

Plans of houses in Capel Street and Charlotte Street approved by the Council.

Seamen's Mission (St James' Chapel) opened at the junction of Ruperra Street and Dock Street.

October

More drownings at Town Dock and accidents (some fatal) throughout Pillgwenlly.

November

Street tramway proposed from Station to bottom of Pillgwenlly.

December

Dennis Caley fined for disturbing a chapel congregation at St James' Chapel, Dock Street.

1871—January

Concert at Girls' School, Church Street, in aid of Mission to Sailors.

Wesleyan Day School given Government grant of £160 which included extra money for proficiency. Mr H J Hopkins and Mr S Wright (teachers) pass first class Queen's Scholarship Examinations.

February

Strike by navvies over length of lunch break at Alexandra Dock construction.

Edward Williams age 13, given twelve strokes of the birch and imprisoned for one day for attempting to steal a knife from Mrs Gray's shop in Ruperra Street.

William Taylor murdered near the "Salutation Inn", Commercial Road. Stabbed to death by a man named Henry Evans.

Jewish Synagogue opened at the junction of Lewis Street and Francis Street.

March

Seamen's Bethel Mission, Williams Street, hold Bazaar. Since opening (two and a half years ago) 2,000 seamen entered and cared for. Upwards of £1,000 left by seamen at various times to be taken care of until their return from sea.

Newport Ragged Schools placed under the control of the Local Authorities School Board.

April

Bazaar held at Commercial Road Baptist Chapel. Rev E Thomas (Minister) tells gathering that money needed to clear large debt.

Pillgwenlly Tonic Solfa Class give a concert at Wesleyan Schoolroom.

May

Impressive Service aboard the "Cashmere" in Town Dock, conducted by Mr Isaac White of the Mission to Seamen. Three hundred joined in the Service—some aboard and the remainder on the quayside. Prayer meeting held in the cabin after Service.

July

Wesleyan Day School, Commercial Road, increase fees because of large number of children seeking entry.

W H Davies, famous Tramp Poet, born in Church Street.

August

Many accidents and deaths caused during construction of Alexandra Dock.

Cherry Fair held at the Cattle Market.

Great Western Railway likely to contribute towards the cost of completing the Alexandra Dock.

September

Accidents (some fatal) common in Pillgwenlly amongst children.

October

Fatal accident at new Dry Dock under construction near Jacks Pill.

November

Spread of smallpox causes concern. Deaths in Pillgwenlly.

December

Tea given by Christian ladies to about a hundred navvies working on Alexandra Dock and Caerleon Railway.

Pill Catholics open a Voluntary School at St Michael Street.

Mary Mahoney sentenced to 21 days' hard labour for stealing a petticoat and other property of Ann Stacey of Castle Street. The articles had been worn by a child who had died from smallpox. Mahoney pawned clothes to buy drink.

1872—January

"United Prayer Services" held in non-conformist Churches in Pillgwenlly.

Death of Mr Crawshay Bailey of Abergavenny, large shareholder in the Town Dock and Alexandra Dock.

Wesleyan Ragged Sunday Schools Annual Treat at Ragged School, Dock Street. Each child given at least one article of second hand clothing.

Jeddo Street residents petition Council about poor street lighting.

Small Pox epidemic receding. Still some deaths. Council order offending premises to be cleansed and lime washed.

February

Pillgwenlly Wesleyan Day School, Commercial Road, congratulated by Government Inspector. School good in discipline and instruction. Infants well instructed in "reading, writing and numbers". Mr Henry Taylor still in charge.

Edward White fined for keeping an illegal slaughter house in Commercial Road.

Overcrowded state of poorer class houses discussed by Council following Small Pox epidemic. Houses described as "overcrowded dens". Special Committee set up to deal with the housing of the poor.

March

Sailmakers cut hours of work to 54 per week.

Mr George Elliott, MP, and Lord Tredegar inspect progress on construction of Alexandra Dock.

April

Council approve houses in Upper Raglan Street.

May

Rev Samuel Fox, Rector of Holy Trinity Church, dies at the age of 45. Came to Newport in 1860 to become Curate of St Paul's. Joined Holy Trinity in 1861. Leaves wife and four children.

Death of Mr Graham, Superintendent of Sailors' Home, Dock Street.

First Iron Screw Steamer to be built at Newport launched. The vessel, christened "Blanche", built at Uskside Works, Church Street.

Suggestion that Rev A R Blundell of St Woolos replace the late Rev Samuel Fox meets with opposition, congregation say he is too "High Church".

Sunday Schools march through the Town and hold Whitsun Fields on Whit Monday.

June

New Dry Dock opened on riverside near Jack's Pill. Called Alice Dry Dock after the name of the daughter of the Chairman of the Dry Dock Company (Mr C Lyne). "Duke of Newcastle" first ship to enter. Band of the 1st Mons Artillery played at function.

Erection of Tredegar Wharf School, Williams Street, commenced.

Thomas Littlejohns, a haulier, killed in Castle Street on his way to Uskside Works with horse and truck. Truck wheels run over his head.

More accidents and deaths during construction of Alexandra Dock.

Sarah Morgan, age 33 of Raglan Street, dies in childbirth. Mr E G Humpage medical attendant sent for trial for gross neglect and inattention.

July

Rev Francis Bedwell appointed Rector of Holy Trinity Church. Appointment gives satisfaction.

Conversazione at Ebenezer (Welsh Calvinistic Methodist) Chapel, near Ebenezer Terrace. Presentation to Mr T H Howell, Organist.

August

First trial trip of Iron Screw Steamer successful. Speed of eleven knots attained.

September

Thomas Haggerty, a Somnambulist, of Castle Street, killed whilst sleep walking going to attend his horse in adjoining stable.

New Mission Church proposed by St Paul's Church at Lewis Street.

Many Beer Houses in Pillgwenlly below standard.

November

Horse drawn street tramways proposed for Newport including Pillgwenlly.

Sailors' Home in Dock Street appeal for funds. Churches asked to take collections.

Outbreak of Typhus causes concern, because of likely spread in overcrowded houses. Tubercular diseases in children also cause concern.

Petty thefts, drunkenness, vice, drownings and accidents amongst the whole society dominate the scene in Pillgwenlly.

1873—January

John Thomas and William Thomas sentenced to six weeks' hard labour for not going to sea aboard the British ship "G L Walters" after signing articles.

February

Newport Gymnastic Club formed in the Cattle Market.

April

Edward Rutter, an open air preacher, charged with causing an obstruction at the junction of Cardiff Road and Commercial Road whilst preaching the Gospel. Mr H Lloyd of the YMCA pleads a case for open air preaching.

May

George Close of Dolphin Street killed at Alice Dry Dack.

June

Sunday School Whitsuntide activities.

Complaint from leaders of the Synagogue about the treacherous conditions in Francis Street and the poor lighting.

American Indian Missionary Nar Kar Wa preaches at Commercial Road Baptist Church in native costume.

Annual Wool Fair at the Cattle Market.

Newport Ragged Schools in financial difficulties. Suggestions that they be handed over to the recently constituted School Boards run by the Local Authority.

July

Wesleyan Day School, Commercial Road, under Henry Taylor, described as one of the best schools in the Government Inspector's District.

Plans of a Foundry in Potter Street approved by Council.

Many drownings in Town Dock and river.

August

Cherry Fair held at the Cattle Market.

Tredegar Wharf School, Williams Street, designed to accommodate 400, opened. Contractor, D C Jones of Gilvach; Architect, A O Watkins. Opened by Lord and Lady Tredegar. Religious service led by Rev F Bedwell of Holy Trinity Church, with his children's choir.

Council's Medical Officer of Health complains of overcrowding. Says that one child in four is doomed to die. It is only the fittest who survive; the weaker ones are killed off in infancy.

Council approve fourteen houses in Lime Street.

Work on construction of Alexandra Dock makes rapid progress.

Dry Dock accommodation being increased.

First horse drawn tramways scheme proposed from Victoria Hall, Bridge Street, to Pillgwenlly. Shares in new Company being taken up rapidly.

September

Financial position of Ragged Schools for destitute children improves.

Complaints about condition of Mountjoy Street and Herbert Street considered by Council.

Newport Sailors' Home, Dock Street, threatened with closure because of lack of funds.

Many child deaths from accidents and diseases.

Eliza Willis, a woman well advanced in pregnancy, killed at Cork Wharf whilst picking up coal to keep her other children warm.

Houses in Upper Raglan Street and Upper Lewis Street approved by Council.

November

Death of Alderman Latch, first Mayor of Newport under the Municipal Reform Act 1835. Also, Mayor in 1845. Respected Pill Businessman and one of the first Directors of the Newport and Pillgwenlly Water Works Company. Proposed John Frost who became Mayor in 1836.

Much crime in Pillgwenlly. Sentences severe.

1874—January

Brig "Malipatres" carrying war material for the "Carlists" (followers of Don Carlos) seized at Nantyglo Wharf.

Fire at Thomas Ponsford's premises in Castle Street. Police Sergeants Wilcox and Winmill and seven Constables get fire engine from Temple Street and extinguish blaze.

Drunkenness in the Police Force causes concern.

One hundred and fifty poor aged and infirm Pillgwenlly residents entertained to a meat tea at the Wesleyan Schoolroom, Commercial Road.

Annual meeting of the Newport Sunday School Union at Commercial Road Baptist Church. Over 200 teachers attend. Schools report success in "teaching children to sing from notes".

March

Contract for laying of track from Bridge Street to Pillgwenlly for horse drawn tramways let to Messrs Arthur Speight and Sons. Track to include Commercial Road, Bolt Street, Dock Street and Ruperra Street.

Council approved houses in Upper Baldwin Street and Inkerman Street (Alexandra Road). Also extension of Commercial Road Baptist Church and erection of Holy Cross School, Lower Cross Street.

Mr J H Thomas (Secretary of State for the Colonies) born in George Street.

April

Kate Prince sentenced to ten days' imprisonment for stealing a flannel petticoat in Church Street.

John Appleby charged with absconding from the employment of his Master Joseph Rogers, a Potter.

May

Benjamin Knight sentenced to six weeks' hard labour for refusing to go to sea.

Council agree environmental improvements in Dolphin Street.

Charles Kirby, four year old child, burnt to death in Baldwin Street whilst playing near burning rubbish on ballast bank.

Council's Medical Officer of Health complains of increased drunkenness. He says "notwithstanding the good times and high wages, you see just as many ragged children running the streets without shoes and stockings as when times were bad. More money in the wages means more beer down the fathers' throats."

Whitsuntide Festivities. Sunday School children parade in the morning and then go to their Fields.

June

Efforts made to save Sailors' Home in Dock Street from closing because of lack of funds.

Plans of new Baptist Chapel to be erected on the south side of Upper Alma Street received by the Council (Alma Street Baptist Church —demolished May, 1976).

Work on construction of Alexandra Dock progressing rapidly.

Annual Wool Fair at the Cattle Market.

July

Annual meeting of Mission to Seamen held in Schoolroom, Temple Street.

August

Houses in Williams Street, Wolseley Street, Upper Raglan Street and Upper Alma Street approved by the Council.

Concern still expressed about lack of accommodation for the working classes. Medical Officer of Health says legislation must be brought in to tackle this most pressing problem.

Albert Hall English Baptist Sunday School (early in 1875 to become Alma Street Baptist Sunday School) celebrate their eighth anniversary.

September

Alleged murder of James Coleman, an engine driver of Frederick Street, in George Street.

Mary Ann Addis, a prostitute, sentenced to one month's hard labour for being drunk and using bad language in Commercial Road. Became so violent that it took two policemen to get her to the Station.

October

Monmouthshire Railway Company block right of way from Cardiff

Road to Herbert Street. Protestors break down gates, and cause a riot.

November

The Working Man's Dwelling Act passed by Parliament.

Council approve houses in Upper Alma Street, Upper Lewis Street and James Street.

December

Trial trip over Newport horse drawn tramways carried out by officials.

1875—January

New Baptist Chapel opened on the south side of Alma Street (Alma Street Baptist Chapel). Accommodation 600. Cost £850. Architect Mr Coomber, Builders Edwards and Holland. Collections at opening services £16 10s.

Much destitution amongst the poor because of bitter weather. Mayor calls a meeting in the hope that "the well-to-do" will help.

Petition from residents of Pillgwenlly to Council to alleviate Brothel nuisance in Dolphin Street.

February

Newport Ragged Schools still see need to remain despite School Board schools being set up.

Horse drawn Tramways introduced into Pill.

Tredegar Wharf School (opened 1873) report satisfactory progress. School full.

March

"The Lord Tredegar" arrives at Newport to be prepared to be the first vessel to enter the new Alexandra Dock when opened.

Efforts made to extend the horse drawn tramways in the direction of the new Docks.

Newport and Pillgwenlly traders get together to arrange to give bread, coal, meat, etc, to the poor in appreciation of the opening of the Alexandra Dock.

April

Henry Taylor, ten years teacher at the Wesleyan Day School, Commercial Road, and said to be one of the first Socialists, appointed Government Inspector's Assistant.

Alexandra Dock opens amongst much gaiety and hilarity. Town brilliantly illuminated.

Holy Cross RC School opened in Lower Cross Street.

Woman named Leyshon severely burnt in house in Potter Street. Fire caused through her being drunk.

Death of Lord Tredegar.

May

Concert at Tredegar Wharf School to raise funds to relieve the poor people of Pillgwenlly.

"Hospital Sunday" in Newport. Many Pillgwenlly Churches take collections to help finances of the hospital.

Usual Sunday School procession and Whitsun Fields.

June

Twenty three ships in New Alexandra Dock, twenty seven in Old Town Dock.

Lad named Jeremiah Foley, son of the landlord of the "Orange Tree' public house, High Street (now St Michael Street) killed whilst working at the Cambrian Foundry.

Annual Wool Fair at the Cattle Market.

Seven year old boy named Henry Pumry drowned in brickyard pond. Pill children use pond in which to swim and bathe.

July

Plans for the construction of Baldwin Street, Jeddo Street and a new street to be called Price Street approved by the Council.

September

Houses in Wolseley Street sold for £147 and £245.

St Stephen's Church Mission Room opens in Watchhouse Parade.

October

Plan to erect the Oddfellows Hall (demolished 1970s) at the junction of Alma Street and Herbert Street drawn up. Probable cost £500.

November

Funeral of PC Turner who received fatal injuries in Portland Street on 5 November whilst trying to calm a bon-fire mob. Subscription list set up to help widow and seven children.

St Michael's School opened in Clarence Street.

Many drownings and accidents throughout Pillgwenlly during the year particularly at the Alexandra and the Town Dock. Crime, drunkenness, vice, etc, still very evident.

Introduction

Before Pill Was . . .

Newport would probably have remained a quiet little market town (and Pillgwenlly would never have been) but for the discovery, in the latter half of the eighteenth century, of great mineral wealth in the hills to the north of the town. It is difficult to imagine that up until 1801 the population of the whole of Newport was only just over 1,000 and at that time what we now know as Pillgwenlly was an uninhabited marshland. The area from Ebenezer Terrace southwards to the River Ebbw at Cardiff Road was six feet lower than the surface of the ground lying to the north, and the only approach was via Stow Hill and Belle Vue Lane to the present railway crossing near Mendalgief Road.

Pill Reclaimed from the Sea

It took many years to import ballast "to reclaim the hollow from the sea". One estimate gives the amount of ballast deposited as 6,000,000 cubic yards. There were no docks, of course, and the ships would discharge their cargoes and ballast at the wharves on the Riverside. Transport of the ballast was difficult—there were no roads until 1810. Even in 1843 the area was described as extremely dangerous. Pits and ravines existed, the area was ankle deep in mud, and not a single lamp existed in the whole neighbourhood. Despite these difficulties the ballast was gradually spread over the whole of the Pillgwenlly area.

Alderman H J Davis in his book *Rise and Progress of Newport* printed in 1891 aptly describes Pill at this time (about 1840). He says "At the commencement of Commercial Road stood the Salutation Inn, but from thence to Pillgwenlly, half a mile, there was not a single house, whilst on either side of the Road (Pill Road—now Commercial Road) were low wet meadows. The first part of the Old Dock (the Old Town Dock) was then in progress, but was not completed until 1842. There were a few houses on the Cardiff Road, but green fields occupied the site of the present Clytha Square, Clytha Crescent, Mountjoy Place and Herbert Street.

The opening of Old Town Dock in 1842, of the Cattle Market in 1844 and the extension of the Old Town Dock in 1858 caused many houses to be erected in the Pillgwenlly district, whilst the conversion of tramways into railways, the formation of the Pontypool and South Wales Railways and the construction of the Alexandra Docks, caused a rapid increase in the population and tended to the prosperity of the Town."

The Canal

The mineral wealth to the north of the town led to the construction of the Monmouthshire Canal southwards to terminate at the Town Pill—just south of Newport Bridge. The first recorded historic event in Pill appears to be about 1805 when the Canal was extended through what was at that time a vast area of marshland to Dock Parade, near the end of the present Church Street. The Canal was opened in 1812.

The Tredegar Wharf Company

Sir Charles Morgan, Bart, was responsible for much of the early development of Pill (as indeed of the whole town). Sir Charles (described at the time as the most perfect remaining example of "the fine old English gentleman") was Chairman of the Tredegar Wharf Company which consisted of himself, Samuel Homfray, Mrs E Homfray, Rowley Lascelles and Thomas Fothergill. It was this Company who between 1807 and 1810 constructed Commercial Road (then known as Pill Road).

Origin of the name "Pillgwenlly"

The Pill Road terminated near the same terminal point as the Canal —near the Pill level crossing, locally known as Pill Gates where in 1902 the Tredegar Dry Dock was established. This point was a natural place for early development particularly as nearby was a large water inlet known as "Pillgwenlly"—from which the area derived its name. "Pill" being another way of describing a water inlet or harbour and "Gwenlly" a corruption of Gwynllyw—the name of the old warrior saint of the fifth century who built a church on the site now occupied by St Woolos Church. So Gwynllyw's harbour became known as Pillgwenlly. The Welsh name "Gwynllyw" has after many corruptions finally assumed the name of "St Woolos".

Roads

The only other roads in the area about this time appear to be Potter Street, Ruperra Street, George Street, Cardiff Road and Mendle Gief Road (Mendalgief Road). Also there were some tram roads which circumscribed the area and had the dual purpose of road and railway. These traversed George Street, Cardiff Road and Courtybella Terrace. All these roads were in a deplorable condition and Commercial (Pill) Road was extremely dangerous.

The Docks

The construction of the Town Dock began in 1835 and the excavation work from these activities helped to reclaim much of the Pillgwenlly Marshes. The Docks opened in 1842 and were extended in 1858. In 1868 work began on the Alexandra Dock which was opened in 1875 (North Dock). The Dock was extended in 1907 to form the South Dock.

The Cattle Market

The site of the Cattle Market in Tredegar Street was originally about ten feet below the level of Commercial Road and was raised by ships' ballast and other materials. It was opened in 1844.

Progress

Following the opening of the Docks and the Cattle Market improvements came about in quick succession. Requests were made to the Shipmasters to discharge their ballast on the marshland which enabled houses to be speedily erected, and builders who could not wait for the ballast built kitchens and cellars below the general level of the new filled areas. The Canal, which had opened in 1812, was filled in and abandoned in 1854.

By 1851 houses had been completed in the streets around the Cattle Market and around the Holy Trinity Church further south in Potter Street. In fact, by this time much of the area east of Commercial Road had been developed but, to the west with the exception of Temple Street, New Street and parts of Baldwin Street, little progress had been made.

More Houses

By 1857 the grid pattern of the streets to the west of Commercial Road (Alma Street, Lewis Street, Williams Street, etc), had been set out and within the next twenty five years most of this area was developed. About this time houses were also erected in the north-eastern ends of such streets as Lime, Jeddo, Baldwin, and Marion, but the development of the south-western ends of these streets towards Mendalgief Road had to wait until the turn of the century. The 1884 ordnance sheet shows this area as being occupied by the Redhouse Farm and the Alexandra Pottery.

Condition of Houses and Environment

Many of Pillgwenlly houses were built with solid walls in dressed coarse stone on the outer facing and rubble on the inner skin. As most of the houses were built on filled land and over the years as settlement took place the heavy stonework fell away from the inner skin, tilting and fractures occurred.

The majority of the houses lacked the basic conveniences like indoor toilets and bathrooms and certainly none had the more modern conveniences like central heating.

The environment was poor and the layout of the area gave a run down and worn out appearance. With no open spaces and masses of terraced houses built in a grid system the overall appearance throughout the area was monotonous and uninteresting.

It was for these reasons that the Council early in 1960 decided that something needed to be done to re-vitalise the area. The question was whether to demolish and redevelop or to repair and improve.

Early Transport

The Early Days

In the early days the only way to get from one place to another in Pillgwenlly was to walk—that is unless you were rich enough to own a horse.

So horse drawn transport became the first means by which some residents were able to move any distance, and to have goods and services delivered to their doors.

The Horse Omnibus Service

It was on the 2 January 1845 that the first serious attempt was made to move people from one place to another in numbers, when Mr George Masters started a horse omnibus service from his wine and spirit vaults close to Newport Bridge to near the entrance to the Old Town Dock. The bus operated four journeys daily and the fare charged was 4d. The service was discontinued twelve monthse later owing to the deplorable condition of the road along Church Street from Commercial Road to the Dock entrance.

Other horse omnibus services were introduced at various times after the withdrawal of Master's bus, but the duration of each was short lived owing to lack of support; the inhabitants apparently preferring to walk, or if they could afford the fare, use one of the many horse cabs plying for hire in the town.

The Horse Drawn Tramways

Horse drawn tramways were introduced in Pill in 1875 by a group of businessmen who formed the Newport (Mon) Tramway Company. Work on the horse drawn tramway was completed in July 1874 but the line was not opened until the 1 February 1875 owing to the delay in obtaining suitable horses. The route ran from Commercial Road at its junction with the Frederick Street railway crossing (locally known as "the iron gates") along Commercial Street, to Tredegar Place (now Bridge Street) to Station Street near the Queens Hotel. It was intended to continue the line to the end of Commercial Road to terminate near the second railway crossing near Church Street (known locally as "the wooden or "Pill Gates"). But this plan was stopped by the powerful Tredegar Wharf Company who claimed ownership of the road and denied access over it. The consent was eventually given in May 1876 and the tramway extended to the end of Commercial Road in December 1877.

A loop line had also been constructed running through Ruperra Street, Dock Street and Bolt Street where it joined the main line again on Commercial Road. This loop line had been constructed mainly to deal with the activity created by the Town Dock which was opened in

1842, but with the opening of the Alexandra Dock on the 13 April 1875, and the consequential decline in trade at the Town Dock the loop line was discontinued and closed in 1877.

Conditions in Commercial Road at this time are described in the *Monmouthshire Merlin* of the 19 March 1886 under the heading "Fatal Termination To Tramcar Accident" which reads:—

"Thomas Smith of 19 Capel Crescent who was knocked down by the horse of No 4 Tram in Commercial Road on Monday at 4.20 pm died on Thursday night in the Infirmary. There were at the time of the accident two tramcars on the road; the one going up to the town went into the siding, for the other to go down to the terminus. The car had only just started from the siding, and the driver was in his usual position with his hand on the brake. The horse knocked Mr Smith down and trampled on him. The wheel did not go over him. The driver said the man simply stood in front of the tram mesmerised and he had no chance to avoid him!!"

Stables and Car Sheds

The stables in Mountjoy Street also caused problems at this time. The original car shed was in Friars Field (on the site now occupied by Fussells Sports Shop in John Frost Square) and in 1886 this was replaced by a car shed and stables in Mountjoy Street next to the Gospel Hall. Sunday was the day for cleaning out the stables and the smell brought much protest from those attending Church!!

Rivalry

At this period there was much rivalry between the private Companies running the horse drawn *bus* services and the horse drawn *tram* services resulting in bankruptcies. In March 1894 Newport Corporation purchased the horse tramways from Newport (Mon) Tramways Company for £4,500. The tramways were then leased to the South Wales Property, Machinery and Carriage Company for an annual rental of £1,860. This Company which was owned by Solomon Andrews & Sons commenced operating the service on 30 July 1894 on a lease which could be terminated by either party at the end of seven, fourteen or twenty one years. It was terminated on the 30 July 1901 and on this date Newport Corporation took over the operation of the horse tramways with a view to electrification of the system.

The Electric Trams

9 April 1903 was an important day for the people of Pill (and indeed for all Newport residents) for on this day the first electric tramway route was opened by the Mayor, Councillor J H Dunn. The route was from Pill Gates, Commercial Road to Corporation Road (Lysaghts Works). The fare was two old pence (2d).

On the 3 December 1917 the service was extended to Alexandra Road up to the entrance of the Alexandra Docks.

No Sunday Trams

No trams operated in Pill (nor, in fact in Newport) on a Sunday until May 1922. The question of Sunday trams had been raised first in 1903 and a number of times afterward, but following ratepayers' polls and opposition by the elected Councillors, the union and the workers, the pressure was resisted until on the 28 May 1922 when the peace of Pill on Sunday was shattered by the rattling wheels and clanging bells of the noisy trams.

The Last Tram

The trams remained a part of Pill until the 5 September 1937 when the last electric tramcar (No 51) left the Docks terminal at 10.50 pm for the Corporation Road Depot. A large cheering crowd assembled in Westgate Square to witness the departure of the tram, overloaded with passengers, who, during the journey stripped it of anything that could be kept as a souvenir. It was a sad day for many Pill residents who had travelled in the trams for thirty four years. Later in the same year No 51 tram returned to Pill to be broken up at the yard of John Cashmore Ltd.

The Buses

So on the 6 September 1937 the bus service as we know it today commenced in Pill.

Horse Drawn Deliveries

Many of the older Pill residents will recall having their milk, coal, bread and greengroceries delivered by horse and cart and indeed even remember their loved ones being taken to their last resting place by the same means. Trips to the lighthouse were enjoyed despite the slow, bumpy journey in often overcrowded carriages. Those who could not afford to go by horse and cart would cycle—some on the old "Penny-farthing boneshakers".

The Car

Since the end of the second world war many Pill residents have had the luxury of a car, but many still use public transport, and although the horse has disappeared the cycle can regularly be seen on the streets of Pill.

Churches and Other Religious Communities

Introduction

An entry in the Rev John Wesley's diary dated 19 October 1739 reads:

> "I preached in the morning at Newport (Mon) on "What Must I Do To Be Saved" to the most insensible, ill behaved people I have ever seen in Wales. One ancient man, during a great part of the sermon, cursed and swore almost incessantly and towards the conclusion took a great stone, which he many times attempted to throw."

Some thirty five years later (on the 28 August 1775) Wesley again preached in our town and it is interesting to read the entry in his diary on that occasion:—

> "I reached Newport about eight and soon after preached to a large and serious congregation. I believe it is five and thirty years since I preached here before to a people who were then wild as bears. How amazingly is the scene changed!"

At this time, of course, Pill was covered by water, but when early development commenced, places of worship figured prominently amongst the building. In this section we trace the history of the Pillgwenlly Churches from the Mariners' Chapel built in 1827 at Mariners' Wharf near the present George Street Bridge to two completed in the present decade.

Ebenezer Welsh Presbyterian (Commercial Road)

Calvinistic Methodism

This Church has its origins in the great Methodist revival in Wales during the eighteenth century when Whitefield, the two Wesleys and Howell Harris stirred the spiritual life of the country, but it was not until 1800 that Calvinistic Methodism had a permanent abode in Newport.

In that year a meeting was held in the Castle Yard when the Rev David Jones, Vicar of Llangan was the guest preacher, and a Church of twenty nine members established. The Church met for a while in an old Malthouse which was most unsuitable and eventually moved to a Chapel called Hope Chapel between Corn Street and Skinner Street, the Pastor at that time being a man named John Rees. In 1814 the Chapel was forced to close as the deeds were held by one of the Deacons who went bankrupt. The creditors unmercifully seized the building and sold it to help recoup their losses.

The Church on the Move

The Church was, therefore, compelled to seek another place to worship and after leaving "Hope" went to a room adjoining a bakehouse at the bottom of Stow Hill opposite St Mary's Church and it was here that Morgan Howell, later to become one of Wales most famous preachers, began to preach. The next move was to the Old Castle where they remained for five years.

Language Problems

At this time there appeared to be some language and theological problems which caused some difficulty resulting in the Welsh Methodists procuring a plot of land from the Tredegar Estate "in the rising suburbs of Pillgwenlly at the head of the new Turnpike Road leading to Cardiff" and here they built a Chapel which they called "Ebenezer".

The New Chapel

The *Monmouthshire Merlin* has preserved for us the following appreciative notice of the Chapel in its issue of the 17 October 1829:—

> "The large and handsome Chapel building at Newport by the Welsh Methodists is nearly completed and will we understand be open for Divine Worship in the course of a fortnight. It is the largest place of worship in the Town, though there are as many as seven Chapels here."

The Trustees at that time make interesting reading. They were Henry Jones of St Mellons (Minister); Morgan Evans of Pillgwenlly (local Merchant); Henry Lawrence of Pillgwenlly (Agent); William Evans of Pillgwenlly (Blacksmith); David Lewis of Newport (Carpenter); John Stedman of Newport (Carpenter); Morgan Howell of Newport (Minister); William Lloyd of Newport (Shopkeeper); Morgan Thomas of Islwyn (Farmer); William Howells of Machen (Minister); Edward Edwards of Bassaleg (Farmer).

First Service

At the opening service on the 1 November 1829 one of the special Preachers was a Baptist from Cardigan, the Rev John Herring—a very tall thin man, but possessing an abundance of ready wit and general humour. On one occasion when crossing the mountains to Merionethshire to the Chapel where he was to preach, he is said to have met the great Baptist divine Christmas Evans. "Well well, what a surprise to find Christmas in the middle of summer" said Herring. "How, now," retaliated Christmas Evans, "No greater surprise than to see a herring on top of a mountain." Such was the ready wit of those Preachers so long ago.

The Debt

The huge debt pressed heavily on the small Church and the Rev Morgan Howell took on the job of collecting the money. He travelled

North and South Wales mounted on his little pony preaching in many Methodist Chapels and making appeals. Crowds flocked to hear him preach and many would refuse to take money in their pockets fearing his persuasive powers. He finally collected £1300—£600 in the south and £700 in north Wales.

Ministers

The last Minister was the Rev T Emlyn Evans and previous Ministers have included Rev Rees Jones (Cardigan), Rev B D Thomas (Llandeilo), Rev John Davies, Rev John Lewis and Rev D H Williams.

Church Closes

In November 1982 the members were faced with a colossal sum for repairs which they were not in a position to meet and so the Church closed and the congregation moved to share accommodation with the Presbyterians at Stow Park on Stow Hill.

Wesleyan Methodist Chapel—Commercial Road

The Barracks—Mill Parade

The first recorded facts about this Church are found in some reminiscences of the late Mrs M E Honeywill of 7 Temple Street in 1924, when on the 21 December she reached her hundredth birthday. She tells how her father Thomas Beavon, a great Methodist Leader came to Newport very early in the 1800s and preached to the people of Pillgwenlly in a rented room at the Old Barracks on Mill Parade (later to become Isca Foundry). He became known as "the Bishop of Pill" and through his preaching the Wesleyan Methodist Church at Commercial Road was formed in 1832. She tells how one dark winter's night she had an urgent message for her father who was preaching at the Old Barracks and went along only to be challenged by a sentry, and had it not been for the intervention of an officer, she in her tongue-tied fright would have been shot!!

Church Re-modelled

Little was known about the Church at this time, but in 1832, the Chapel at Commercial Road between Potter Street and Church Street was erected and occupied, but the *present* building built in Norman style is the one erected in 1849. In 1898 important alterations were carried out and although the front and outer walls were left, the internal arrangements were entirely remodelled and renewed with the exception of the Old Galleries which were left. The organ was removed from the Commercial Road end of the Chapel to the opposite end and the schoolroom was built at a new level.

Disastrous Fire

At 4.40 am on Monday 17 February 1908, following the Sunday Evening Service when there was the usual large congregation, a tragic fire broke out at the Chapel and it was completely gutted. The work which was completed in 1898-99 had to be done all over again, the damage being estimated at about £2,000. Undaunted the members quickly arranged for the work to be done and it was not long before the Chapel, which accommodated nearly 1,000 people, was again ready for their worship to the God they loved.

Church Day School

It is interesting to note that the first Voluntary Day School in Pillgwenlly was set up by this Church in 1847. It was situated at the rear of the Church and accommodation was for boys and girls who were taught reading, writing, arithmetic, etc. The building still exists today, and can be seen from Clarence Street.

Decline

In common with most of the Pillgwenlly Churches, this Church had much blessing until the time of the second world war (1939-46) when the decline set in. It struggled on until 1957 when it closed and later was used as a builder's store, and so one of Pillgwenlly's earliest Churches which had been God's instrument for saving many souls was no more.

Mother Church

The Commercial Road Church was the Mother Church of Price Street Methodist Church, and when she "died" she bequeathed to "her daughter" the fine pipe organ to which thousands of Pillgwenlly residents had sung for over a hundred years. When the daughter "died" in 1978 it was the wish of the members that the organ remained in the area and was passed on to the St Stephen's Church who have incorporated a part of it in their splendid organ.

The Welsh Baptist Church, Commercial Road
(Deml Eglwys Y Bedyddwyr)

Two Welsh Churches

It was unusual that in a comparatively small "English" town like Newport during the last century there were three Welsh-speaking nonconformist Churches, and most unusual to find that two of them were in Pill—"Ebenezer" at the junction of Cardiff Road and Ebenezer Terrace and "the Welsh Baptist Temple" in Commercial Road between Alma Street and Mountjoy Street.

Small Beginnings

Like most of the Churches in Pill, the Welsh Baptist Temple was born through prayer, when brethren from the Commercial Street and Charles Street Baptist Churches joined the few Pill Welsh Baptists in prayer using houses in the neighbourhood.

Chapel Built

Gradually the work grew, and after leasing a piece of land in Commercial Road from the Tredegar Wharf Company, the foundation stone for the Church was laid on the 7 August 1843. By June the following year the building, which measured fifty one feet by forty one feet with extensive galleries and a large Sunday Schoolroom in the basement, and which cost £1,000, was erected.

Opening Services

On the 25 and 26 June 1844, at the opening services, the Baptist Temple was filled to capacity with no less than eleven Ministers officiating. The Church was constituted with eighty four members and with Mr T Morris late of Pontypool as Pastor. Most of the Services were conducted in Welsh, but as time went on English was used during evening worship.

Pew Rents

Amongst the Offices listed in a Church publication of 1903 was "Conductor of Singing" which one would expect to find in a Welsh Church, but another—"Pew Rent Collector" one might perchance to find in Scotland rather than Wales!! The average annual pew rent was one shilling. Another interesting entry in the Annual Accounts for 1903 was a donation of ten shillings to the local hospital.

Decline

At the beginning of the century the Church flourished but following the aftermath of the 1904 revival and the decline of the use of the Welsh language in Newport, the membership decreased and the building began to fall into disrepair. For some years it remained empty and in the mid 1960s was demolished to make way for a petrol filling station, leaving "Ebenezer" as the only upholder of the Welsh language in Pill. Ebenezer itself closed in 1982 and so the Welsh language was lost to the area.

New Testament Church of God, Commercial Road

Bible Christian

This Church in Commercial Road near the Alma Street junction is at present used as a Pentecostal Church by the West Indian Community, although it must be said that no one is barred from worshipping here. The Church was originally built and used by a denomination known as "Bible Christian" which was born out of the great growth of the Methodist family. The denomination saw its inception in 1815 in the sparsely populated area of North Devon, the founder being a William O'Brien whose evangelistic efforts commenced the movement. His labours were continued by a James Thorn, who became to the Bible Christians what John Wesley was to the Wesleyans.

Small Beginnings

When the Bible Christians came to Newport in 1843 they conducted their services in a house in Queen Street off Cardiff Road, and in 1849 a Chapel was built on the present site near the corner of Alma Street. Worship continued in the Old Chapel until it was condemned as unsafe in 1881 when the present building was erected and opened in 1883, to accommodate 600 people.

Prayer

The Church appeared to have a very fundamental, strict and bible based doctrine, believing very much in the power of prayer. The 1889 Newport Directory lists the Minister as Rev W Jeffrey of 10 Daniel Street and says that the Sunday Services started with a prayer meeting at 7.30 am!!

In 1892 the membership was 170 and the Sunday School had 320 scholars with 35 officers.

Back to Methodism

In 1907 the Church appeared to have adopted a more orthodox Methodist theology and was called the United Methodist Church.

Bethel Temple

In the 1950s to the early 1970s a Pentecostal Group took over the building and for some time is was known as Bethel Temple (Assemblies of God). After receiving much blessing in this building the fellowship moved to a larger and more central building in the Old Wesley Methodist Chapel in Stow Hill where they remain to this day, holding their last services in Pill on the 8 September 1974.

It was with much sadness that on the 25 April 1983 the Rev Eric Dando, who had started the work in Pill, and continued it at Stow Hill, having built up a large and prosperous Church, passed peacefully into the presence of his Lord. He was apty described as the "Prince of Pastors".

New Testament Church of God

The Church remained empty for a while but was eventually taken over by another Pentecostal Group known as the New Testament Church Of God. This Group commenced in Newport in 1968 with five members, and after holding prayer meetings in homes, they moved to the Boilermakers' Hall in Church Street, to Crindau School, to "Belle Vue School", to Albert Street, to the YMCA in Commercial Street and finally settled in Commercial Road where they are today.

Holy Trinity and St Stephen's Churches

C of E's Lag Behind

Before the opening of the Holy Trinity Church in Potter Street in 1852, the only accommodation for Church of England Services in the rapidly developing Pillgwenlly area was a small schoolroom belonging to the Tredegar Wharf Company in Temple Street. Other denominations like the Welsh Presbyterians, the Wesleyan Methodists, the Welsh Baptists and the Bible Christians were firmly established in the area, having built their Churches some years earlier. So it was thought that it was about time that the "Established Church" had a place of worship in the district. In any case, the St Paul's Church in Commercial Street was often too full and a "Chapel of Ease" was becoming necessary.

The Site

The site picked, which was at the end of Potter Street off Commercial Road, was described as having a most uninviting appearance, being filthy and neglected. Broken trams, heaps of rubbish and pools of stinking water wallowed in by pigs was a blot on an area which generally was already unattractive. In April 1852 the Architect, a Mr Langdon, instructed the builders, John Hunt and Sons, to clear the site and prepare it for the erection of a new Church at a cost of £2,7000 to be built in the twelfth century English style.

Church Opens

In June the following announcement appeared in the *Monmouthshire Merlin.*

> "The Church recently erected at Pillgwenlly and which is dedicated to the Holy Trinity will, with God's permission, be consecrated and opened for Divine Worship on Tuesday 15 June 1852. The morning sermon will be preached by the Rt Rev Alfred Ollivant DD the Lord Bishop of the Diocese, the afternoon sermon by the Rev Alan Cornwall MA, Rector of Baverston Gloucester and Chaplain to the Queen."

District Church—First Baptism

Once the Church was opened it was decided that it would not be a "Chapel of Ease" for St Paul's Church but a District Church in its own right. The day following the opening there was a little competition for the honour of the first baptism in the new Church. Mr William Morgan a Chemist of Pillgwenlly was the successful competitor, having his son named William *Trinitas* Morgan to identify the boy with the Chapel.

Much Blessing

The Church had so much blessing that in 1884 it became necessary to take the "overflow" from Holy Trinity by building another Church. The site chosen was at Alexandra Road near Adeline Street and the builder was Mr W M Blackburn who later became a Councillor and was made Mayor of Newport in 1909. The Church called "St Stephen" had its origin in Watchhouse Parade where, in 1875, a Mission Room was set up, and in 1884 the members moved into their fine new biulding. For many years both Churches prospered, but in the mid 1900s with the fall in interest of things spiritual, both Churches began to decline and and a decision had to be made to close one.

The Mother Church closes

The axe fell on the Mother Church—Holy Trinity, and the last services were held there on Easter Sunday 1975 attended by the Bishop of Monmouth and the Archdeacon of Newport. There was always a faint hope that Holy Trinity would open again but the building gradually fell into decay, suffered vandalism and soon was beyond repair. When it was estimated that some £80,000 was needed to put it in order (remember it cost only £2,700 to build), it was agreed that demolition was the only answer. The small band of devoted Christians joined the "Daughter Church" and the Church became known as "St Stephens and Holy Trinity".

Holy Trinity was demolished in September 1977 after being closed for two years and the site was purchased by the Family Care Housing Association who erected on it a sheltered scheme for the elderly which remains today. All that is left of the old buildings are the Gargoyles* which have been incorporated into the new buildings on the site.

And they became one

Since the two Churches became one the marriage has been much blessed under the present Ministry of the Rev Brian Stares who came to the area in 1977. A new Church Hall which was opened in June 1974 and dedicated by the Bishop of Monmouth the Rt Rev D G Childs, is much used as is the Church itself. In 1980 the Council sold to the Church a piece of land opposite the main entrance on which in 1982 was erected a fine new Vicarage.

Portland Street Methodist Free Church

Tea Party

The first we hear of this Church in Pillgwenlly was on a Monday afternoon in July 1852 when one of the largest sheds in the New Cattle Market was selected for the occasion of a large Tea Party held

---

*A Gargoyle is a projected rain spout carved in the form of a grotesque figure.

by what were then called the Wesleyan Reformers and their friends.
The object of the Tea Party was to raise funds for a new Chapel in
Pillgwenlly as a further Wesleyan Methodist witness to that existing in
Hill Street in the centre of town. The proceeds of the event together
with the cash in hand amounted to £70.

Expelled

In the *Monmouthshire Merlin* later in the year this group were
referred to as "the Expelled" which implies some sort of break-away
from the mother Church in Hill Street. By September they had
acquired a piece of land in Portland Street and made known their
intentions to erect "a neat little Chapel for themselves and the poor
of the locality". Later in the month, on a Friday afternoon, the foundation stone was laid by the daughter of the Builder, Mr Moore, and
so the Wesleyan Reformers came to Pill. By December the Chapel was
built and roofed.

The Church opens

On Sunday the 20 March 1853 the Chapel was opened. At 6.00 am
members met to implore God's blessing on the Services that would
follow. In the morning and evening the Services were led by a Mr
Langride and in the afternoon the Rev Barfield BA, of Hope Chapel*
delivered a forceful sermon. The collections for the day were £20 and
"the Reformers" had firmly established a witness in Pillgwenlly.

The Church prospers

For nearly a century the Church held a steady witness in the area,
but the 1939-45 war took away many of its men folk and in 1950 the
building closed to become a furniture warehouse, and later a paint
warehouse as it is today.

Fire

In 1978 workmen involved in major repairs to the building following a fire uncovered some commemorative stone plaques laid in 1907
which revealed some of the history of the Church. One was in memory
of a member of the Parry family (James) who were devoted workers
in the Church for many years.

Commercial Road Baptist Church
(previously known as Pillgwenlly English Baptist Church)

"Foundations" Laid

In 1860 a few earnest Christians, desiring to extend the Christian

---

*Hope Chapel stood on the corner of Dock Street and Skinner Street,
where later the Olympia Cinema was built and where now stands Olympia
House.

influence in Pill, got together and met in a Carpenter's Workshop in
Portland Street, loaned to them free of charge by a fellow Christian,
John Northcote, from the Baptist Church at Commercial Street. This
was the start of the Commercial Road Baptist Church. At the head
of this little company was the Rev Evan Thomas at that time Pastor
of the Welsh Church at Charles Street, and under his able oversight
the Church progressed smoothly and successfully.

About this time the Rev Ebenezer Edwards of Llanelly visited the
Town with the express purpose of founding an English speaking
Baptist Church in Pill, and found in the Portland Street mission a firm
foundation for the Church he came to establish.

On the 29 September 1861 he commenced his ministry and immediately gathered people together in increasing numbers. Regrettably,
he became ill soon afterwards and had to resign the Pastorate in
August 1862.

Sunday School

In January 1862 before his resignation, a Sunday School was
formed, the teachers and scholars numbering about forty, the Superintendent of which was Daniel Rees, later to become Church Secretary.

It soon became evident that the little room in Portland Street would
be too small for the ever growing numbers and a move was made to
a larger room in Temple Street.

New Pastor

After losing the services of their first Pastor so quickly, the little
but growing Church were sad, but their sadness was soon turned to
delight when the Rev Evan Thomas of Charles Street Baptist Church,
who had been of outstanding help when the Church was formed,
agreed to accept "the call", and started his ministry in April 1863.

New Premises

As well as a new Pastor the Church at this time were provided with
larger accommodation through Mr Samuel Homfray (a well known
Pill business man) who agreed to Services being held in one of his
large sheds in the Cattle Market. With the growth of the Church
membership (it was now one hundred and five) and the increase in
the number of children attending the Sunday School, it became necessary to take steps for the building of new Church premises.

So, on the 21 May 1863 a contract for the building of the new
Church in Commercial Road was agreed between W M Jones (Builder)
and the Church Officers. The building was to cost £700 but with organ,
etc, the total cost was in the region of £2,000. On the 16 July 1863
the foundation stone was laid by the Mayor of Newport (G W Jones,
Esq) and enclosed were current copies of *The Star of Gwent, The
Monmouthshire Merlin* and *The Baptist Freeman*. A tea for over nine
hundred people at the Cattle Market followed.

By November the Church was completed and on the fifteenth of that month the first services were held.

Membership increases

By the 1 January 1876 the number of Church members had reached two hundred and forty six and by 1877 the Band of Hope numbered one hundred and fifty.

Baldwin and Lime Street Missions

The same year (1877) the Church felt a need to expand its activities to South Pill and consequently set up a mission in Baldwin Street in a room at a rental of 3/- per week. The expanding mission soon outgrew the building and on Thursday the 15 August 1878 a new building in Lime Street built by Brother W M Price and rented to the mission for 6/6d per week was provided. The building was extended the following year at the cost of £10 14s 5d. At this time the number of scholars and teachers in the Commercial Road and Lime Street Branch Sunday Schools numbered seven hundred and fifty. In 1884 the Lime Street mission became strong enough to stand on its own feet, and the members set about securing new and larger premises in which to commence a new and independent Church. The Gospel Hall, Inkerman Street (Alexandra Road), was selected, and so on the 15 October 1884 began what we know today as the Alexandra Road Baptist Church.

The Rev Evan Thomas Retires

At the age of seventy the Rev Evan Thomas found the strain of the ministry too much and in 1888 retired to make way for a younger man —the Rev Benjamin Thomas of Merthyr. Evan Thomas died on the 5 September 1893, his death being hastened by an accident which he sustained when knocked down by a vehicle in the Station Approach.

Dolphin Street Mission

The Church felt a further need to expand its activities and in 1893 set up another mission in Dolphin Street.

The Rev Benjamin Thomas moves to London

In September 1894 the Rev Benjamin Thomas accepted a call to the Harlesden Baptist Church in London. During his ministry the Church had made great strides having a membership of over four hundred, and he was succeeded by the Rev George Evans of Mount Pleasant Church, Blackwood, in September 1895 who remained until 1921.

Church Decline and Closure

From the 1920-30s the Church began to decline, the decline being aggravated by the Second World War when so many of its menfolk left home to see service abroad. In the early 1960s the Church closed and in 1964 following alterations was used as a motor car showroom.

Ministers this century have included the Revs George Evans, W H Williams, D J Thomas, T Roy Jones, W Price Lewis and Frank Downes.

Alma Street Baptist Church
(now Emmanuel Evangelical Church)

"The Upper Room"

This Church began in 1866 when a group of Christians led by Mr J Pardoe Thomas (later to become the first Pastor) met for prayer in the sail loft of his ship chandler's premises in Canal Parade, lit by oil lamps and having for seating accommodation the sailmakers' benches, coils of rope and bales of canvas. It was literally an "upper room" where prayer was wont to be made, and there was "the breaking of bread". Hitherto Mr Thomas had been a member of the Commercial Road Baptist Church but felt led by God to start another witness in Pill following the time, in 1865, when C. H. Spurgeon the famous London Preacher preached to crowds of over ten thousand at the Cattle Market.

Answered Prayer

The prayers from "the upper room" were quickly answered, for this makeshift accommodation was soon inadequate for the growing Church and they moved to more adequate premises at the Prince of Wales Clubroom in King's Street. The Church continued to grow and by 1867 another move was necessary; this time to the Albert Hall in Ebenezer Terrace and the Church was then known as the Albert Hall Particular Baptist Church. By 1872 it was obvious that the Church needed its own and larger premises and in that year a sum of £8 was put aside as the nucleus of a building fund. In January 1873 it was decided to erect a building, the cost not to exceed £600. In fact the new Chapel cost £838 and was opened in Alma Street (between Charlotte Street and Kirby Street) in January 1875.

The Church in the early 1900s

Some idea of what the Church was like at the turn of the century is told in a Church magazine of September 1962 in an article written by the then oldest Church member the late Mrs Annie Pring. She says:

"My first memories go back to about 1887, when taken to the Infants' Class. The Leader was Mr Chris Thomas the son of the Founder and first Minister of the Church. It was held in a little room with no organ nor piano, and we sang Sankey's hymns led by the Leader. Later I was promoted to the Senior School and I can still remember him teaching us to recite passages of Scripture, with his beautiful mellow voice. The only heating was from a big stove in the middle of the room and the singing was accompanied by the harmonium.

From the earliest days we were always working hard for some
alteration or extension to the Church. Mr Fred Jones had built up a
very good choir which formed the basis of the Newport Choral
Society of which he was conductor, and their early rehearsals were
held in the School Hall."

(Mrs Pring died in April 1983 in her hundred and second year whilst
this book was being written.)

Blessing, Decline, and Blessing Again

Alma Street Church was one of the first Churches to catch the spirit
of the 1904 Revival, and meetings were held every night of the week,
continuing until 10.30 pm with singing, prayer, and testimony, always
packed to the door.

During the period about 1930-60 the Church fell somewhat into
decline and little blessing was evident except during the period 1941-49
when many of the menfolk were away at the war and the Rev B J
Allsopp had a hard but successful ministry. The one bright spot in
the 'Thirties was the sending of one of its men to the Mission Field
in the Congo where the Rev Wallace Arr gave his life in a brief but
precious ministry in Bolobo. Since 1960 the Church has known much
encouragement. Three of its members are at present on the Mission
Field, and the Church attracts large congregations including many
young families and overseas students.

The "Daughter" Church

Alma Street Baptist Church has always had close connections with
the Alexandra Road Baptist Church, arising from the time when the
latter Church found themselves in financial difficulties in the early
1900s and called on the Alma Street Church for help. One member
recalls an incident when in a Church meeting the Church Treasurer
of Alma Street (Mr Maybury) stood up and reported that he had
bought a Church at an Auction Sale for something like £500. That
Church is now Alexandra Road Baptist Church. He asked for workers
to help keep it going and this help was quickly forthcoming. The two
Churches worked in close association until about 1930 when Alexandra
Road once again became independent under the ministry of the Rev
D W Ingram. It is fitting that the present Secretary of Emmanuel
Chapel (Mr Jeff Nowell) is the son of the late Mr Joe Nowell a
Deacon and faithful worker at Alexandra Road for many years.

The Fire

In July 1966 a considerable part of the Church buildings were
ravaged by a mystery fire which destroyed the large school hall and
damaged much of the chapel and other buildings.

The Old Church closes

The last Services were held in the Alma Street Baptist Church on

the 25 April 1976 when the Rev Graham Harrison (the Pastor)
preached to about two hundred and fifty people. After singing the
Doxology, the congregation dispersed and the doors closed for the
last time after over a hundred years of witness in the building to be
continued in new and more pleasant surroundings. The old Church
building was demolished in May 1976 being part of the massive
Pillgwenlly redevelopment.

New Church
The present Church building, which was erected in 1976-77 at Rutland Place, opposite the Royal Gwent Hospital, is one of the most
modern in South Wales. Equipped with parking facilities, and designed
to cater for the disabled it possesses a modern computer organ and
many present day amenities. Since it opened on the 12 November 1977
it has known much blessing.

Ministers
Previous Ministers have been: Rev J Pardoe Thomas; Rev J
Meredith Jones, Rev Griffith J Harris, Rev Edward Elliott, Rev H
Luther Jones, Rev B J Allsopp, Rev John Bennet. The present Minister
is the Rev Graham S Harrison MA BLitt, who has been in charge
of the Church since 1962.

Mountjoy Gospel Hall

Lost in the Mist
The Mountjoy Street Assembly began its history some time before
1876 when a company of Christian Brethren met in Pill, but before
that date the story is lost in the mists of the past. The first factual
statements were recorded by the late Mr Williams Richards who was
very much the founder-father of the work on the present site.

Portland Street
He records in his diary that at one period a number of people used
to meet in an upper room somewhere in Portland Street. Although it
is not clear where this room was, it was probably the same carpenter's
loft used at a different period by the Christians who started the
Commercial Road Baptist Church, owned by fellow Christian John
Northcote and situated on the right hand side of Portland Street near
Commercial Road. William Richards stresses that besides the happy
times in proclaiming the Gospel, the high delight of the week was to
gather for prayer on a Sunday evening after the Gospel meeting, and
his diaries tell of the rich times spent in fellowship with God which
sometimes ran late into the night.

Mountjoy Street
It was on the 1 March 1876 that the Church was established in

Mountjoy Street and over the years much blessing and growth has been evident. On two occasions it was enlarged, and as the Sunday School grew, two adjoining cottages were acquired for use as class-rooms. During the 1920-30s the Sunday School was several hundred strong and in the 1930s the "Mothers' Meeting" had over two hundred ladies on the register.

Titles

Over the years the Assembly seems to have had different titles. In 1889 it was called "Christians' Meeting Room" and in 1877 and 1893 was listed as "Bethesda Brethren", then reverted to "Christians' Meeting Room" and in the late 'Twenties and early 'Thirties became known as the Mountjoy Gospel Hall, which name it retains today.

Broadcast Services

Broadcast services have been held on three occasions, in 1958, 1962 and 1970.

Missionaries

During the life of the Church three of their members have been called to the Mission Field. One to Italy, one to India and one to South Korea.

Redevelopment

The Church building was originally included in the redevelopment programme, but was excluded on instructions from the Ministry. At that time there was some disappointment as members felt it was an opportunity to rebuild the existing old building, but it was not to be.

New Building

However, in 1981 a decision was made to rebuild without the help of the Ministry or the Local Authority and the Brethren took on the responsibility, under God, of financing and constructing the new pre-mises themselves. On the 21 June 1981 the last services were held in the Old Gospel Hall and whilst the new building was being erected the fellowship moved to temporary accommodation in the YMCA in Commercial Street. In October 1982, the Brethren moved back and on the 13 November the building was officially opened when large congregations assembled to hear two old friends of the Assembly, Mr Stan Ford of Bournemouth and Mr B Osbourne of Dinas Powis, preach the word of God.

Alexandra Road Baptist Church

Beginnings

Alexandra Road Baptist Church owes its beginnings to the nearby Commercial Road Baptist Church who with "missionary vision" set up, in 1877 and 1878, the Baldwin and Lime Street missions. In 1884 the Lime Street Mission became strong enough to become independent and large enough to need new premises, and it was on the 15 October 1884 that they took over the Gospel Hall, Inkerman Street, Alexandra Road, which became what we know today as Alexandra Road Baptist Church.

Difficulties

The Church seemed to prosper for some years but very early in the 1900s things went so badly that it was necessary to call for help from the Alma Street Baptist Church. This Church responded readily and took responsibility for the work at Alexandra Road, which involved the purchase of the building as well as its maintenance and spiritual oversight. In 1907 the Church was called Alma Street Mission.

New Hall

With the coming of the Rev D W Ingram to the Church in 1923 things began to improve and at the beginning of the 1930s it was decided to replace the old army hut which had been used to accommodate the various Church organisations. No money was available to employ a contractor so the members set about doing the job themselves with the help of many non-church members like the men at Braithwaites who supplied and erected the steel frame. Three Church Officers who spent many hours supervising the work were Mr J Beddis and railwaymen John Cloake and Joe Nowell, all being commemorated by plaques outside the Church. The hall was finished in 1938 and immediately taken over by the Army and the Church did not get use of it until the end of the Second World War.

The Rev D W Ingram

The Rev D W Ingram who ministered from 1923 to 1947 was one of the most loved and well respected people in Pill—so much so that he earned the title of "Bishop of Pill". It was under his guidance that the Church once again became strong enough to "go it alone" and in 1939 it regained its independence.

Boys Brigade

A history of Alexandra Road Baptist Church would not be complete without a mention of the Boys Brigade which has been strong and active in the Church for over fifty years. The founder of the Brigade was Jim Essery another well known figure in Pill whose good work has been carried on by such men as Alan Manley, Stan Hayward, George French, and in more recent years, Clive Gibson.

Decline

Despite the more recent Ministries of the Revs Cyril Thomas, W J Howell, Keith Feltham and David Hardiman the Church has not prospered but is kept open by a small faithful congregation who will soon be celebrating one hundred years of witness in the area.

Price Street Methodist Church

The Spirit Moves

During the latter half of the nineteenth century Methodism spread through Newport like an uncontrolled fire, and by the turn of the century a dozen or more places of worship had been built and were filled with people seeking God.

"Basham's" Chapel Started

By 1885 there were already two Methodist Churches in Pillgwenlly, but not satisfied with this the Methodists took steps to provide for the needs of the Alexandra Dock district. A meeting was held in the Commercial Road Wesleyan Methodist Chapel (between Potter Street and Church Street) on Wednesday the 28 January 1885 when it was explained that it was hoped to build a Chapel to accomodate three hundred and fifty persons at a cost of £500 in the Price Street area. So enthusiastic were those at the meeting that almost half of the amount required was given before the meeting closed. One interesting donation was that of Mr Basham who gave £10. The Basham family were to become leaders and benefactors in the Church for many years to come and Pill residents knew the Church as "Basham's Chapel". The Bashams ran a thriving Drapery Store in Commercial Road near Portland Street for many years and was a household name in Pill. In fact, the shop is still referred to as "Basham's" although it changed hands over a decade ago.

Memorial Stones

On Monday afternoon the 1 June 1885 the ceremony took place of laying eleven memorial stones in the new building, which was in course of erection at the corner of Price Street and Pottery Terrace. Each stone bore the name of a worker in the Methodist Denomination in Newport and each laying was accompanied by a gift of £10 by the person whose name was on the stone. During the speeches which followed it was said that "The Methodists had selected a populace neighbourhood in which to erect a Mission Chapel and Sunday School." The Sunday School would be built first and used for public worship until the Chapel was finished. The Architects were Habershon and Fawkner, the Builder a Mr Price, and the cost of the building £730.

Opening Services

By August 1885 the Chapel was completed and the Opening Services were led by the Rev J Stringer of Cardiff. During the Services it was announced that the Commercial Road Wesleyan Methodist Chapel had taken a leading part in raising funds for the new building and it is interesting to note that the close ties between the two Churches remained firm. When Commercial Road closed, they gave to Price Street their fine pipe organ and the Communion Rail.

Blessing and Decline

Older Pillgwenlly residents can remember the Chapel being filled to capacity each Sunday, with a large sisterhood, a huge Sunday School and a thriving Boys Brigade.

Gradually, the numbers dwindled and the enthusiasm for the Lord's work diminished. When the redevelopment of the area was announced in the 1960s and the people began moving away from the area things became critical. At first the building was included amongst those to be pulled down. Then moves were made to retain it, but eventually, early in 1978 it was decided that the best course was demolition.

Final Services

Later that year, on the evening of Friday 11 August a Final Service of Praise and Thanksgiving was held when the Rev Douglas O Field BA, and the Rev David Howarth BA, BD, MLitt (Minister), conducted the services and the address was given by the Rev Wyndham Bold who had been Minister of the Church for many years.

After the singing of the final hymn "Who is on the Lord's side?", the following prayer repeated by the whole packed congregation echoed through the decaying building:

"As we leave this place, grant us Your peace,
Peace with you O God; peace with each other,
Peace within ourselves, through Jesus Christ our Lord.
Amen."

Demolition

Within weeks the bulldozers moved in and the Chapel which had served the people for almost a century had gone. In 1982 the site was planted with grass and trees to remind those who were not perhaps touched by the witness of "Basham's" Church that God in nature still exists in all His sovereignty.

St Michael's Roman Catholic Church, Clarence Street

The Great Famine

The Great Irish Famine in 1846-47 caused a large exodus of people from the Irish shores and between 1845 and 1855 some 7,000 to 8,000 immigrants came to Newport, many of them to the Pill area. They came to Newport partly because there was already in existence an established Roman Catholic Church with Residential Priests.

The First Catholic Church in Newport

It was in 1809 that the Rev Barnes began to say Mass in a room over the shop at the corner of High Street and Market Street. In 1812 the Rev Ealey built a small Chapel just outside the West Gate which sufficed until 1893 when it was pulled down to make way for the present St Mary's Church.

The Church in Pill

By 1869-70 many Roman Catholics had settled in Pillgwenlly and to educate the children three houses were purchased in High Street (now St Michael's Street) and one was fitted out as a Chapel. The other two were handed over to the Trustees as a school on the 1 September 1871. This house/church was the humble beginning of the Parish of St Michael, Pillgwenlly and Father Bailey one of the Priests at St Mary's, Stow Hill, was given the responsibility of overseeing the work in Pill.

At first Mass was said in the School Chapel, but Father Bailey saw the need for a Church building for the ever growing Roman Catholic community and set about raising money for its erection. Weekly collections in the area brought in large sums and several heavy drinkers "signed the pledge" that they may give more towards the building of the Church!!

Truly St Michael's Church can be called the Church of the poor, for coal trimmers, iron shippers, and others freely and willingly gave their time and labour to help dig the foundations. Others who were out of work gave the whole day. Thus the foundations were dug, almost without expense.

After much hard work the Church was built and opened in 1887.

Father Hill

The first Residential Rector came to the Church in 1921 and remained until his early death in 1926. He was Father Hill, a converted Jew. He was a worthy successor to Father Bailey and his sudden death in 1926 was partly due to his heavy labours in the service of his people.

During and after the war he raised over £14,000 for new schools and the Father Hill Memorial School at Oswald Road was named after him. Father Hill was followed by Father Burris and Priests in more recent years have included Rev J G Fevez, Rev W Davies, Rev A E Holland and the Rev Joe Hassett. The present Priest is Father Troop who returns to Pill having served St Michael's between 1960 and 1965.

St Peter's Church for Seamen, Temple Street

Fine Building

This fine Church building which graced Temple Street for nearly a hundred years was demolished early in 1981. It was in the mid 1880s that Sir George Elliott, the MP for Newport (and others) bought a piece of land in Temple Street in order that a Church and Institute for Seamen, their wives and families, together with a Chaplain's Residence, should be erected. The Church which was opened on the 18 January 1889, was called "St Peter's" and the attached Home for Seamen, which was erected at the sole expense of the late Sir George Elliott, was named "Elliott Home for Seamen".

The first Chaplain was the Rev W W Garry who, after serving the Church for many years died on the 19 March 1908. In 1923 the Church became a Registered Charity, the Trustees including the Bishop of Llandaff, and the then Mayor of Newport, a Pill Councillor, Edward Davies of 25 Cardiff Road, himself a prominent Churchman, an ardent Trade Unionist, and an important worker in the cause of temperance.

Worship

Worship was held every Sunday and was attended not only by Seamen calling at the Alexandra Dock, but by many residents connected with the sea. The Church bell would call to worship the retired seamen, the pilots, the tugboat men as well as other residents living in their small terraced houses surrounding the Docks.

"Halfmast"

Following the Rev W W Garry, other men like the Rev Atkinson were "called" to minister to the Seamen and residents and perhaps the best known was the Rev Molyneux who, together with his wife had a particular interest in children and young people. Another Chaplain whose name is believed to be French was affectionately known in the area as "Halfmast" because he wore his trousers well above his ankles!!

Active Church

The Church was very active, not only on Sundays but during the week as well, when youth clubs and concerts were held in the evenings and the annual Sale of Work was always eagerly awaited. One of the residents who attended the Church was the late Miss Agnes Bagg who lived opposite at No 2 Temple Street. Before her recent death she told how her father, Richard Bagg was a Sidesman and brother William pumped the organ and tolled the Church bell. To do the latter he had to stand on a chair with a rope in each hand and perform a balancing act!!

Hostel

Many Seamen stayed at the hostel where they could not only have meals but sleep. They were cared for by Mrs Borge and Mrs Dickenson who were well known in Temple Street. Two maids and a house-keeper were also employed.

Church and Hostel close

Through the 'Thirties and early 'Forties the Church survived but eventually closed. In 1948 the building was sold to the Monmouthshire Territorial Army and for a decade it was used as a TA Drill Hall and Centre. In later years it was used as a warehouse but fell into disrepair until it was demolished in 1981 to make way for a car park.

St Barnabas' Mission Church, New Ruperra Street

Origins

This Church had its origins in the St Pauls' Church in Commercial Street when, at the time of the 1904 Revival it was felt that a Mission Church should be established further south in the Pill area. Consequently, a piece of land in New Ruperra Street was leased from Lord Tredegar and on the 10 May 1906 the foundation stone was laid by him.

After a short service in St Paul's Church, a procession, headed by the band of the Naval Brigade and which included Viscount Tredegar and the Mayor (Councillor John Liscombe) marched down Commercial Street to Commercial Road and on to New Ruperra Street where the foundation stone was duly laid.

Church opened

The Church was opened and dedicated on the 6 October 1906 when there attended the Bishop of Llandaff, Lord Tredegar, and the Vicar of St Pauls, the Rev A A Matthews. The Bishop paid tribute to Mr Matthews and his large, able and willing workers who had seen the need to extend the facilities for Divine Worship in the Parish of St Paul. The new Church had been built and only £200 was required to make it free from debt.

Decline

The Church prospered for a number of years and, in addition to the Sunday Services, regular mid week meetings such as Band of Hope, Temperance and Bibles Classes were held, but after the 1939-46 war the enthusiasm began to decline. Eventually the building fell into disuse and in 1964 was taken over by a Printing Firm and remains so today.

Other Churches

Other Pillgwenlly Churches and Missions which warrant a brief mention include:—

1   The Mariners' Church
This would seem to be the very first Church in Pillgwenlly opened in 1827 for the Seamen calling at the River Wharves. It was situated at Mariners' Wharf where now stands the George Street Bridge. It was used as an unsectarian Church until about 1870, but afterwards was only used by the Scandinavians for their Services.

2   The Seamen's Bethel, Williams Street
This Church seems to have taken over the function of the Mariners' Church before 1870 and did much good work amongst the seafaring population of Pillgwenlly. It was situated in Williams Street immediately behind the Commercial Road shops.

3   The Mariners' Friendly Society
This was another Christian Organisation which did much good work amongst the seafarers. They opened premises in 1891 at Wolseley Street (between Nos 8 and 10) called the Sailors' Chapel or the South Wales Gospel Mission.

4   The Mission to Seamen
But the largest and most consistent work amongst the seafarers was done by the Mission to Seamen who originally set up in 1871 at the junction of Ruperra Street and Dock Street (St James' Chapel), and remained there for some eighteen years until the St Peter's Church and the Elliott Home for Seamen opened in Temple Street in 1889. From that date until 1951, the spiritual and physical needs of the Seamen were met by this Church, but in that year a move was made inside the Alexandra Docks where the Church remains to this day.

5   The Navvies' Mission
This was formed by the Church of England in 1877 with the object of stationing a "Missionary" wherever large public works were in progress. It was the "Missionary's" duty to preach the Gospel, conduct a night school, promote temperance meetings, and adopt other means of improving the moral welfare amongst Navvies. As there was much public works going on in Pillgwenlly towards the end of the 1800s and the beginning of the next century, "Missionaries" were sent to the area. One of the places they operated from was the Old Police Station

in Temple Street where a certain **Mr J P Evans**, who lived at 92 Alma Street, did some excellent work amongst the Navvies in 1910. He had much success in his work, which was to get the Navvies to abandon drink, bad language and ungodly living, to pray night and morning and to keep the Holy Sabbath Day. A daunting task!!

6   Small Missions

There have also been many small Missions in Pillgwenlly, like the Churchman's Bible Class at 44 Portland Street, the Baptist Mission Hall at the junction of Potters Parade and Portland Street, the Mission Church at Dock Street and others that have come and gone.

Suffice it to say that God has worked in Pillgwenlly since the first soul arrived there and is still working today. Other Institutions have come and gone but the Word of God and His Church go on for ever.

The Jewish Synagogue, Francis Street

Early Records

The earliest records preserved by the Newport Hebrew Congregation give the date of its foundation as the 6 March 1859. On that day a few far-sighted orthodox Jews met in a house in Llanarth Street in the centre of town which served as a temporary Synagogue. Within ten years of its foundation, the congregation had become so firmly established that plans were put in hand to build a Synagogue in Pill.

Foundation Stone Ceremony

The foundation stone was laid on Tuesday the 3 May 1870 on land at the junction of Lewis Street and Francis Street. In front of a large gathering the ceremony was performed by the Rev Mr Ritterberg, the Rabbi, assisted by Mr Jacob Druiff and Mr Abraham Isaacs—the latter performed the actual laying of the foundation stone with an inscribed silver trowel. Psalms 127 and 150 were read in Hebrew followed by a prayer for the Royal Family.

The building cost £800. The Architect was a Mr B Lawrence and the builder a Mr Chack.

Synagogue opened

On the 14 March 1871 the building was opened and consecrated by Rabbi Dr Herman Adler then Chief Rabbi of the British Empire. The community in Pill flourished and it was not long before the services were enriched by the introduction of a choir. "Hanukah" (The Feast of Lights) was celebrated in a joyous spirit with well organised concerts preceeded by the distribution of prizes.

Nathan Harris Memorial Hall

With the building of the Nathan Harris Memorial Hall in Queens Hill and the economic depression of the 1930s, the Jewish community found it impossible to maintain two buildings in the town. The Francis Street Synagogue was, therefore, sold and used as a Tea Warehouse, and the capital derived from its sale used to convert the upper floor of the Nathan Harris Memorial Hall into a Synagogue. It was demolished in 1973 as a part of the redevelopment programme.

The Mosque (or Mohammedan Temple)

First Mosque

Newport's first Mosque was established nearly thirty years ago on the 5 August 1954 when the Head Sheik of the Muslims in South Wales came to Cardiff to perform the official opening at 26 Ruperra Street. It soon became the centre of worship for the town's sizeable Muslim group of which all the men were seamen headed by Mr Akmed Hasser. In more recent years another building was similarly converted in Alexandra Road and these two buildings were sufficient for the small Muslim community in Pill.

Immigration

Following the Second World War one witnessed a large influx of visitors from overseas who came to settle in this country and amongst these were many Muslims. They were attracted to "the working class" areas and some settled in the Corporation Road area where another Mosque was established, but many came to Pill and quickly outgrew their existing facilities for worship.

Dispute

It was not until the late 'Seventies and early 'Eighties, when serious overtures began to be made to the Council for a larger Mosque in Pill. Eventually after many meetings a site was agreed upon in Commercial Road opposite Ruperra Street not far from the original Mosque established in 1954. After all the problems had been resolved between the Muslim community and the Council, the Muslims began to have differences between themselves and it was not until early in 1982 that the differences between the Sunni and Shia sects were resolved, resulting in the opening of a new Mosque available to all Muslims in July of that year. The adapted two storey building is the first stage of the development and later it is hoped to develop the vacant site adjoining. In November 1982 the Pakistan Ambassador, His Excellency Mr Ali Arshad, visited the Mosque at the invitation of the local community.

The Cattle Market

Misnomer

As one looks into the history of Pillgwenlly one realises that the title "Cattle Market" is a misnomer, for this establishment has been used for many more purposes than the sale of cattle. It was established and built by the late Sir Charles Morgan, Bart, and the Tredegar Wharf Company at their own expense, and opened in 1844. It was described at that time as having an area of four acres and accommodation for 1,500 horses and cattle, 2,000 sheep and 500 pigs, with 1,300 feet of shed accommodation. Market day was and still is every Wednesday and it was considered for many years to be the second best Cattle Market in the country.

The Churches

But its use as a Cattle Market for nearly a hundred and forty years has been restricted normally to Wednesdays and much use has been made of it for other purposes not only by the Pill residents, but by Newport people generally and indeed by folk much further afield.

In the mid 1800s the growing Churches of Pill which had started with a few Christians meeting together for prayer in any available building, found temporary refuge in the cattle sheds as they outgrew their accommodation, and remained until they were able to build their Churches. Additionally, the Gospel was proclaimed in the open air by such famous preachers as C H Spurgeon who preached to many thousands in 1865. When the Commercial Road Baptist Church laid the foundation stone of their new Church on the 16 July 1863 over nine hundred people sat down to tea in the Cattle Market following the ceremony.

Sport

The Sporting Fraternity were not slow to realise the benefits they could derive from the use of the Cattle Market. In July 1900 Councillor Clifford Phillips fired the first shot to open a Rifle Range in one of the covered buildings and rifle shooting continued for many years.

George Setterland, one of Pill's well known boxers (who now lives at 302 Lewis Close) tells how he fought in the open air and how, when the weather was not suitable, a cattle shed was cleared, a boxing ring erected and seating accommodation provided for those who wished to see the well known boxers of the day.

Other Activities

If space permitted one could go on—the Annual Newport Dog Show, the Wool Fair, the Gymnasium Club, Circuses, Rifle Shooting, etc. On Christmas Day 1915 the Mayor used the Cattle Market to distribute 220 hot pots, 200 joints of meet, and loaves of bread to the poor.

The National Eisteddfod

But of all the events which took place in the Cattle Market there was none to reach the heights of August 1897 when the Welsh National Eisteddfod was held, not just in Newport, but in Pill and of all places in the Cattle Market for a whole week!!

The only time the Eisteddfod had been held in Gwent previously was in 1350 under the patronage of Ifor Hael at Gwen-y-Cleppa (now known as Cleppa Park).

For this ancient and popular event with all its tradition and culture to be invited to Pill must have been beyond belief and the people of Newport and Pill responded to the challenge. The Pill people opened up their homes to accommodate the many visitors and competitors. Bed and breakfast was available for four shillings per person per night in many Pill homes. The Churches responded as was revealed in one of the Eisteddfod Minute Books when Mr Nicholas of the Alma Street Baptist Church Choir was appointed on the Choir Committee which included many eminent choristers.

That year the Crown was won by a Bard called Mafonwy for a poem on *Arthur Y Ford Gron* (Arthur of the Round Table) and the Chair by Job for an ode on *Brawdgawrch* (Brotherly Love).

Petticoat Lane

In more recent years (much to the annoyance of some of the local traders) the Cattle Market has been used as an Open Air Market where, on certain days of the week, temporary stalls are erected and one can buy anything from a needle to a sack of potatoes.

Relocation

Over the years and particularly in 1973, when the Cattle Market was affected by redevelopment, discussions have taken place with a view to its relocation, so that the land could be used for another purpose. Because of the cost and other factors nothing has materialised and despite the smells, the noise and the occasional stray bull running around the streets, the residents seem resigned to the fact that the Cattle Market will remain their neighbour for many years to come.

Tradition

Like the Transporter Bridge, the Cattle Market attracts many people to Pill, and it has such a wonderful tradition, that, like the Bridge, Pill would never be the same without it.

Coronation and Belle Vue Parks

Coronation Park

Up until 1910 Pill possessed neither parks nor playing fields, simply because the area had developed so rapidly with houses and other buildings essential to its prosperity, that there was just no room left for such amenities. In December 1909 the Council felt it about time that the people of Pill at least had some playing fields and a proposal was accepted to develop some land outside the area near Stephenson Street with access via the Transporter Bridge which had been opened three years earlier. This park was originally called Pill Park and later renamed Coronation Park.

Not Ideal

Although not ideal, at least the people of Pill, including the schools, had somewhere to play their rugby, soccer, baseball and cricket, and it was a place where the children could go to get rid of their surplus energy instead of annoying their neighbours by playing in the streets. The trouble was that, once in the park, if the wind was high, or the Bridge had a mechanical failure, you were left high and dry on the other side of the River Usk—so near and yet so far from home. One could (if one had the nerve) go over the top, but to climb two hundred feet up step by step, and the same distance back down (if you weren't blown off the top) needed much energy which often was not there after a full seventy minutes of rugby or four innings of baseball.

Belle Vue Park

But, although separated from Pill by Cardiff Road, there was always Belle Vue Park which was brought into existence by the critical unemployment problem and the generosity of Lord Tredegar in the late 1800s. In 1891 the Local Government Board sent to all municipalities a recommendation "that they should alleviate the present distress arising from unemployment by promoting works of public utility". Special facilities, like loans, were available to local authorities who took up the proposals, and Newport was not slow in accepting the Government's generosity, particularly as about this time Lord Tredegar was to give away some of his land to the Council. At a banquet given by Alderman H J Davies in 1891, when his fiftieth year on the Council was marked by the Alderman's election as Mayor for the second time, his Lordship announced "that it was his intention to present to the Town a piece of land about 23 acres in extent between Waterloo Road. Cardiff Road and Belle Vue Lane".

Round Table Field

Hitherto this land had been known as "Round Table Field" because of a legend that it was one of the places where King Arthur and his knights used to meet. There was a well nearby and it was a welcome place for them to refresh themselves. When he was made Mayor in 1917 Alderman William Evans, who was born in 1876, remarked "When I was a boy the present Belle Vue Park was called Round Table Field and it was a recognised playground for the children."

The Park Constructed and Opened

Having been given the land the Council set about requesting tenders for its layout and design, and a certain Mr T H Mawson a landscape gardener of Windermere was not only successful in his tender, but given the job of supervising the construction and layout of the Park. The first sod was cut on the 3 November 1892 and memorial trees planted by Lord Tredegar and Alderman Davies. After two years and the spending of £19,000 (£7,000 more than the estimate), the Park was formally opened on the 8 September 1894 by the Mayor, Mr Fred Phillips.

The Lodges

It is interesting to note that the two Lodges, one at the Cardiff Road entrance and the other at Friars Road were built from the stone excavated from the park during the construction. Both remain today and look as strong as the day they were erected.

The Gorsedd Stones

One of the first and most important events ever to take place in Belle Vue Park (regrettably forgotten with the passing of time) was the Ancient Bardic Gorsedd performed on 3, 5 and 6 August 1897 at 9.0 am each morning when the Welsh National Eisteddfod was held in the Cattle Market that year. This Gorsedd of Bards is generally regarded as a relic of the Druid Times and is named in Welsh Triads as the highest assembly of the Isle of Britain. It is held in the open air, "In face of the Sun—the Eye of Light" and the proceedings are carried on within a circle marked out by twelve unhewn stones placed a few feet apart. In the centre is a large stone, also unhewn called the "Maen Llog" or "Logan Stone" upon which the Arch Druid stands facing east. At each of the twelve stones a Bard is placed to guard the sacred circle, and there are others within the circle to take part in the proceedings. The ceremony usually takes about an hour. These stones are still in this beautiful park for all to see today, but perhaps few know their significance.

The Tea Room

Unemployment never seems to go away. It was still a problem in 1910 and was instrumental in the Tea Room being erected. To help the unemploymed the Council agreed to pay for the materials and the wages were paid for by a local philanthropist and so the Tea Room was built.

The Views—the Enjoyment

Many Pill (and Newport) residents have delighted in the charming views of the Bristol Channel, the Severn and the Somerset coastline and hills from this lovely park with the Transporter Bridge towering over the River Usk. Others (sometimes numbering 8,000) have enjoyed the band concerts performed by such eminent musicians as the Welsh and Scots Guards and other local bands, whilst the more religious will remember the hundreds who gather around the bandstand to sing their favourite hymns. During the holidays the children of Pill would take their bottles of water (they could not afford "pop") and their bread (and perhaps butter or jam) and enjoy a picnic on the grassy slopes with the colourful Peacocks hanging around for the bits with which the hungry Pill children could rarely oblige.

Memories

Regrettably, with the coming of the car and the curse of television, fewer people visit this beautiful park and the days of band concerts, hymn singing and the peacocks are but dying memories of those who are reaching the eventide of their lives.

The Schools

Education in Newport can conveniently be divided into five periods:

1 Post 1839—Voluntary schools set up under the National Training Schools Scheme.
2 Post 1871—Formation of schools under the School Board for Newport following the passing of the Elementary Education Act.
3 1904-1918—After the passing of the Balfour Act in 1902.
4 1918-1944—Following the passing of the Fisher Act in 1918.
5 1944-1954—Following the passing of the Butler Act in 1944.

First Pillgwenlly Schools

The first schools in Pillgwenlly were the Voluntary ones, started under the National Training Schools Scheme founded in 1839. These schools were maintained by public subscription to which Sir Charles Morgan, Bart, was a magnificent contributor. They were supported by voluntary contributions from the Churches and other philanthropic bodies.

Wesleyan Voluntary School, Commercial Road

The first individual school in Pillgwenlly was opened in 1847 by the Wesleyan Methodists. Previously in 1832 they had erected a Chapel in Commercial Road between Potter Street and Church Street, and before the premises were rebuilt in 1849 they constructed a small building at the rear (near Clarence Street) for use as a Boys' School. It cost £220 to build and was for "the education of Wesleyan Methodists and others".

The first Master was a Mr William Morgan who, by 1849, was highly gratified with the proficiency in reading, writing, mental arithmetic and grammar. In 1871 a certain Mr Henry Taylor was the Master. Taylor, who was reputed to be one of the earliest Socialists, had a wonderful power and influence over the Pillgwenlly children. He was also the Superintendent of the Wesley Sunday School in Commercial Street (where Boots now stands).

The Trinity Voluntary Schools

The second voluntary school to be established in Pillgwenlly was in Temple Street in a building which was being used for worship by the Established Church, known as Trinity Independent Chapel. (The building still exists and was later used as a Sunday School and Church Hall for Holy Trinity and St Stephen's Churches. It is used today as a furniture warehouse.)

The school opened in August 1854 under the authority of Mr Butt (Master), Miss Bush (Mistress) and Miss Newman (Infants) who had the job of looking after 86 boys, 79 girls and 38 infants. By the following year the numbers had increased considerably and the Infants (numbering 125) were moved to a building in Church Street. By 1856 further increases necessitated the erection of another building and the site chosen was next to the Infants School in Church Street to which the girls were transferred, leaving the Temple Street School solely for boys. Perhaps the most famous pupil to be educated at this school was W H Davies, the Tramp Poet.

One of the conditions of belonging to the schools was that every scholar had to attend Sunday School—not necessarily belonging to the Established Church, but to a Sunday School of any denomination. They all paid a few coppers per week for their education. The building was used amongst other things as the Junior Temperance Society and the Pillgwenlly Children's Missionary Association.

The Roman Catholic Voluntary School

The third Voluntary School was opened by the Roman Catholic Church in 1871 to educate some of the many Catholic children who had settled in the area. Three houses were bought in High Street (now St Michael Street); one was used as a Church and the other two adapted for educational purposes. Each child paid two pence per week to attend and the school started with eighteen scholars.

Voluntary Schools Close

These schools closed in 1900 when the pupils were transferred to the Local Board Schools.

The Tredegar Wharf School

The fourth and last Voluntary School to be set up under the National Training Schools Scheme was the Tredegar Wharf School in Williams Street which was opened by Lady Tredegar on the 18 August 1873. This was by far the largest school in Pillgwenlly with 291 mixed and 148 infants. By 1889 the pupils had increased to 668; 80 children crammed into classrooms only large enough to take less than half that number.

The school was rebuilt in 1934 and extended in 1971.

This school today has a large number of immigrant children, and when celebrating their centenary in 1973, it was reported that eighty or more West Indian and Pakistani children attended the school.

The Roman Catholic Schools

(a) St Michael's, Clarence Street

In 1875 the Roman Catholic Authorities erected a school in Clarence Street to accommodate almost 1,000 pupils. This school still operates today and takes its name from the adjoining St Michael's Church. It was remodelled and re-opened on the 12 October 1898.

(b) **The Father Hill Memorial School**

In 1930 the Father Hill Memorial School in Oswald Road was opened and remained open until June 1974 when the 570 pupils of the St Joseph's Primary School (as it was then called) transferred to the St Joseph's Comprehensive School near Tredegar House, Cardiff Road.

Father Hill, after whom the School was named, was a well-known character in Pillgwenlly amongst both Catholics and Protestants. By his efforts most of the money needed to build the school, which was designed by Mr Cyril Bates, the Newport Architect, cost £12,000, was raised. Father Hill died exactly four years to the day after the school was opened, and it is said that his untiring efforts to establish the school led him to an early grave.

The School is now used as a Sports Club and the HQ of Ushiro Judo Club.

(c) **Holy Cross School**

Although not strictly in Pillgwenlly, a record of Roman Catholic education in Pillgwenlly would not be complete without a reference to this school where many of its children received their tuition.

The school had its beginning in 1874 when a Mr J A Herbert of Llanarth gave the site in Cross (now Emlyn) Street for the erection of a school, and the building costing £672 10s 10d, was opened on the 5 April 1875. The school was extended in 1894 by the addition of a large infants' section and an assembly hall.

In 1936 the school was completely re-modelled at a cost of £17,000 to accommodate 444 children and was opened by Lord Tredegar in one of the worst downpours of rain witnessed for a number of years.

The School Board

The Newport Schools Board first met in 1871, the year following the passing of the Elementary Education Act, and set up the following additional schools in Pillgwenlly:—

1883 **Alexandra,** Pottery Terrace (290 boys, 265 girls and 328 infants). The school was demolished in the early 1970s.

1885 **Bolt Street** (448 boys, 355 girls and 378 infants). This school which is of Gothic design and built by William Price at a cost of £4,000 remains today.

1891 **Spring Gardens,** Courtybella Terrace (300 boys, 300 girls and 305 infants). In November 1924 the Town Council were of the opinion that the children of Pillgwenlly were not getting the same educational facilities as children in other parts of the town, and it was said to be a disadvantage to be born in the area. It was, therefore, agreed to make Spring Gardens a Central School and it was re-named "Belle Vue" in 1925.

The school remains today and takes the name of the demolished Alexandra School.

Some Old Traditions, Street Life and Recollections

Christmas Puddings and Thatcher's Brewery, Alma Street

The Bristol Brewery

Thatcher's Bristol Brewery was established in Alma Street near its junction with Herbert Street well before the turn of the century to brew beer for the thirsty population of Pill and Newport. As a part of the process of beer brewing, there was in the building a large steaming chamber used to clean the beer casks, and early in the 1900s the Company opened its doors in December of each year to hundreds of Pill and Newport housewives offering them the facility to use this steam chamber to cook their Christmas puddings. Right up until a few days before Christmas residents could be seen carrying their cloth-clad china pudding dishes, knotted at the top, enclosing their favourite recipe into the hop-smelling brewery where they would be labelled and duly steamed to be collected a day or two later.

Tradition

As the years went by it became a tradition for the Pill (and Newport) residents to take their puddings to Alma Street and more than 25,000 were cooked at the Brewery each year. Few residents would think of buying "ready-made" Christmas puddings, and few would consider cooking them at home, for it was far easier to take them to "Thatcher's" and what was more important they tasted much better having been cooked in the environment of beer brewing!! In any case, it only cost 6d per pudding.

The Tradition Ends

For more than half a century the Pill and Newport housewives were able to use Thatcher's Brewery at Christmas time, but Christmas 1959 saw the end of the tradition, for later the following year (on the 15 October 1960) the Brewery, then owned by Mitchells & Butlers, moved to Mill Parade.

At the farewell party in the Old Brewery when about forty members of staff drank the final glass of beer, Mr E H Bennet the General Manager said: "It is a service that we offered to the public for many years and we are sorry that the service had to end. I am sure it will be missed".

Recollections of Mrs Honeywill of 7 Temple Street
when she was 100 years old on the 21 December 1924
(born 1824)

"Water was derived solely from the wells and these were regarded as a very valuable asset, indeed so precious was water that it was, as far as possible, used over and over again. For example, water used for toilet purposes or for the washing of clothes was carefully stored to be used for house cleaning. Never, if it could be helped, was water thrown away until it had been used two or three times.

The principal well in Pill was opposite the Ship Hotel (now Alexandra Court—corner of Mill Parade and Alexandra Road). In times of drought Pill people would often queue for hours and sometimes it was necessary to go to other wells at Thomas Street or Baneswell.

On washdays the women of Pill would go down to the Canal (the one running through Pill which was filled in in 1854) near its entrance to the Town Dock and there do their washing in company. This was done to conserve water supplies and to avoid fatigue in fetching water from considerable distances.

The quality of the water in the Newport wells varied considerably and that from Pill's Well and Banes Well were most esteemed for drinking purposes.

It was this water that was hawked through the streets by Ben Davies a Chartist (who only had one arm) and Solomon Meaker. The water was contained in a large barrel on a cart drawn by a horse and sold for $\frac{1}{2}$d or 1d per pint according to the size of the receptacle. It was only drinking water that was sold in this way.

Most of the houses had stone floors and were scrubbed and rubbed with a piece of bathstone, while the hearths were chalked. Bathstone and chalk were sold by hawkers. Sometimes pieces of chalk were found in the ballast thrown out from the ships in the river and these were prizes eagerly sought after.

One of my sons, Samuel, was killed by a tram in Temple Street. In those days horse drawn trams would run along the tram lines carrying ballast from the ships anchored on the river banks to the Mendalgeif Road area through Temple Street.

I can also recall the area on which the Alexandra Dock was built when it was a farm with a toll gate at the entrance."

Recollections of William Evans, Mayor of Newport 1917
(born 1876)

"Take the lower part of town. From Ruperra Street down there was no houses except one which they called "The Halfway House", and the people of Pill regarded themselves as quite a separate Community.

There was no water supply and the people depended upon public wells. There was Pill Well, Springfield Well, King's Hill Well, where

Clytha Square now stands. There was a pump at the top of Cardiff Road and another in Baneswell and people went to the wells and pumps for water unless they bought it from the old man who went around with a barrel and cart selling it as so much a pitcher."

Recollections of the Rector of Holy Trinity Church in 1924

"Pillgwenlly in its historical setting occupies the premier position in the growth of modern Newport. This is due to the foresight and enterprise of a body of business men known as The Tredegar Wharf Company. These men in 1807 procured two hundred acres of land in the locality of the seaditch known as Pillgwenlly. They constructed the first roadway between the cluster of houses built near Pillgwenlly and the town centre, and in every possible way developed the new district.

The hamlet was named after the place name Pillgwenlly. In Welsh the name is self explanatory "Pil" (spelt with one l) means a seaditch, and Gwenlly is corrupted from Gwynllyw, the name of the wild warrior chieftain who owned the Pill and on whose land the seaditch was situated. The extended hamlet carried its name."

Recollections of Wm Parry of 15 Price Street
who celebrated his Golden Wedding in May 1930
and was a Lifelong Teetotaller (born about 1860)

"Here is a picture of Pill fifty years ago (1880): Dock Street—all fields; site of the Temperance Hall—a big field; Baldwin Street and Jeddo Street—all gardens; Lime Street, Price Street and Courtybella Street—a big brickyard; Commercial Road—a chemist's shop, a bakery, two houses, and one or two more shops, the rest fields.

I worked in a Pottery in Pill from six in the morning until ten at night and earned six shillings per week.

On Guy Fawkes night a crowd would steal a boat, set it on fire and drag it through Pill. One night Police/Sgt Turner tried to stop them but he was knocked down. They sat him in a chair in the street and he died.

Election nights were worse. They used to fight like mad dogs."

Recollection of "Gran" Watkins of 24 Courtybella Street
when she was 100 years old on 29 October 1938
(born 1838)

"I have been totally blind for sixty seven years as a result of an accident and have lived for seven years in this same room. I was married at St Mary's Roman Catholic Church to Jehoida Watkins who was once turnpike keeper at the Old Bridge Gate and at the Waterloo Gate, Cardiff Road. I have had eight children, two of whom I have never seen."

Recollections of George Colbourn
who joined the Police Force in 1883 and retired in 1910

"I can remember patrolling from Beaufort Wharf to Cork Wharf when all were working and the Old Town Dock was nearly full of sailing vessels (mostly foreign).

In King's Parade were dancing houses attended by foreign seamen and English girls.

The 5 November was the occasion to set a small boat alight and drag it through Pill and through the town.

Before the Fire Brigade was formed the Police attended all fires with a hand pump and leather hose. When the Town Hall was being built we had quarters in the Albert Hall, Stow Hill, and upon a fire breaking out, the Officer on night duty would go out on to Stow Hill and ring a hand bell which previously belonged to the Town Crier."

* * *

Street Life

An account of Pillgwenlly's past would not be complete without some reference to street life for the activities of a rich and varied boyhood have long since disappeared from its streets.

Gangs

Belonging to a Street Gang was attractive and exciting. One was only admitted after passing rigid tests, but once admitted to full membership a new boy found a wealth of thrilling experiences awaiting him. No member of a gang would dare "split" on another member and if set upon by a rival gang had to utter a particular cry for stalwart support to be ready at hand. He was always initiated to all the rituals and mysteries relating to "luck". At the appearance of a white horse he formed with a wetted finger a cross on the toe of his boot (if he was lucky enough to possess boots) and wished. Or if a gentleman appeared with a straw brimmed hat, the wetted right thumb touched the palm of the left hand and was wiped dry with the clenched right fist before wishing.

Games

But perhaps it was the games that made street life most fascinating. There was marbles, of course, played in the middle of the road until the traffic relegated it to the gutter or the unmade rear black earth lanes. It had a vocabulary of its own, unknown to the intellectuals of the time.

"A taw" was a particular prized marble; "menders" a term used by a player who wished to remove an obstacle from the path of his "taw"; "putsies" was a term used when the taking of another marble was made easy; "caggy-handed" was a term used by a boy who played with his left hand.

Fun or Keeps

Then there was the question of playing for "fun" or "keeps". Some of the more skilful players never played for fun as it was their vowed intention to go home with their pockets filled with their opponents' marbles only to sell them back the following day at the going rate—usually ten for a penny. Many of these Pillgwenlly boys became some of Newport's most successful business men!!

Bogies

"Bogies"—a box on four wheels generated much fun. Great was the rejoicing when a Pillgwenlly mother got beyond the age of child bearing and discarded the pram which for years she had used to push one child after another around the area. The superstructure was replaced by a sturdy wooden box begged (or stolen) from the grocer, and so a handsome vehicle was created. Senior members of the gang were pulled through the streets by "junior entrants" and the few hills in Pillgwenlly were put to good use.

"Follow My Leader"

"Follow my Leader" was a popular game in Pillgwenlly because of the massive heaps of rubble and the immense stacks of timber and ore left about in the area of the Docks. Jumping from timber to timber or stone to stone needed much courage and skill and involved considerable risk especially when the leading boy was athletic and experienced.

Other Games

Then there were the numerous other games: (all played without equipment or equipment which cost nothing). "All the way to London"; "I'm the King of the Castle"; "Leap Frog"; "Jackstones"; "Conkers"; "Hop, Skip and Jump"; "Hop Scotch"; "Knocking up Ginger"; "Dickie Show Your Light"; "Strong Horses Weak Donkies"; "Gaining" (played with a rolled-up newspaper); "Whips and Tops"; "Tag"; "Statues"; "Hoops"; "Catty". Then there were the games played on home-made stilts and others with cigarette cards. One could go on, but to describe all these games would fill a separate book.

Poor Substitute

Today the Pillgwenlly children have most of their games organised for them with Community Centres, Sports Fields, and Clubs being the order of the day. In some respects they have had taken away from them the creative instincts and skills which, for many years, helped to build up the characters of the young.

The Transporter Bridge

New Facts and Photos

Much has been written about the Transporter Bridge so an attempt has been made in this book to publish some facts and photographs which have not been available before, or have not been produced for a very long time.

Vital Statistics

However, it would be wrong to omit the vital statistics. These are:—

24 June 1902: Tender of Alfred Thorne of Westminster accepted.

Autumn 1902: Work commenced.

12 September 1906: Bridge opened.

Cost: £65,672

Span (centre to centre of Towers): 645 feet.

Clear opening between faces of piers: 592 feet.

Clean headway from high water to underside of span: 177 feet.

Height of towers (above level of roads): 242 feet.

Surface to be painted: 1 7/10's acres (74,000 sq ft).

The car holds 100 foot passengers and 8 vehicles.

Masonry in each of the anchorages weighs about 2,000 tons.

Car takes about 1 minute to cross the river.

Origins

The Bridge owes its origins to a man named Fausti-de-Rienzi, a Dalmatian and a great engineer of his time (the seventeenth century). His invention is described in an old volume in the Bibliothèque Nationale of Paris and tells how he designed an ingenious means of access, without using a boat, to an island believed that of Calypso. His apparatus was constructed of simple ropes and could carry four persons at a time.

About 1871 the idea was taken up by an English engineer—a Mr Smith of Hartlepool. His idea was to establish communication by means of a rigid girder between Middlesbrough and Port-Clarence, but through lack of capital, or because the project was not considered feasible at the time, nothing came of it. From these two men M Arnodin (the designer of the Transporter Bridge) got his inspiration and by 1889 he accomplished the task of bridging the mouth of the River Nervion at Bilbao with a single span of 163 metres—the first instance in the world in which the system of the Transporter had been employed. Before coming to Newport he had built another five Transporter Bridges at Rouen, Bizerta, Rochefort, Nantes and Marseilles.

Opposition

Whilst the Newport Council agreed that there was need for a second river crossing, it took some years before a decision was made to erect the Transporter Bridge. As far back as 1869 the problem was approached and for twenty years it troubled the minds of the progressives. Mr R H Haynes the Borough Engineer had seen and studied the Transporter Bridge at Bilbao and recognised its peculiar fitness to meet the needs of Newport. It was eventually agreed to send a delegation to Rouen where another of Arnodin's bridges was nearing completion. So there was organised a never-to-be-forgotten trip to that city on the Seine on the 2 August 1899, and the following day our "city fathers" enjoyed the experience of crossing a river on a Transporter for the first time. Aldermen Jones and Canning acted as interpreters to the designer of the Bridge (M Arnodin) who, despite all his skills, could not speak English, and the idea was accepted by the Council. Parliament agreed and on the 8 November 1902 the foundation stone of the western anchorage was laid by the Mayor Ald H G Davies.

Fascination

From the day work began it was a fascination for those who watched it. First the sinking of the foundations through the alluvial mud to the resisting marl, till at last the finished masonry piers stood above the high water level; then came the gradual building up of the steel towers. When both were finished came the raising of the cable and when all the cables were up and anchored, the public noted how the main girder grew day by day from the centre of the cables, till at last it stretched from side to side. Next came the building of the stiffening girder, followed by the construction of the travelling frame or trolley on the girder of the Bridge; last the slinging of the travelling car, and on the memorable evening of 31 July 1906 the first trial run.

Few Accidents

It is worth recording that during the four years it took to construct this monument of engineering ingenuity, no life was lost and the few accidents which occurred were of a trivial nature.

More Debate

Even after the Bridge was opened the debate about it in the Council Chamber did not cease. When the question of the charge for climbing over the top was considered, Councillors felt that if people took the trouble and used their energy to do this, they should go free. During the debate Councillor Dr McGinn (a Pill Councillor) retorted "It is worth 6d to climb over the top and the Council should pay people for doing it!!" If residents were reluctant to climb over the top there was certainly no hesitation in their using the car for in the four days after the opening 43,000 fares were taken.

Long Life

The Bridge has served the people of Newport (and especially the Pill residents) for over seventy five years and as a tribute to its long service the Mayor (Councillor Les Knight) together with other Councillors and Officers paid a special visit to the Bridge on the 12 September 1981 on its Seventy fifth Anniversary.

Many Pill residents have a great affection for the Transporter Bridge which has for a long time been the only real link between Pill and the other side of the river. It has not only been a monument but a landmark of beauty and utility. If it were to go, Pill would not be the same without it.

Street Names

Unique System

Since the end of the last war the Newport Borough Council has adopted a unique system of naming Council streets, so that it is easy to know where a particular street is situated. For example the Alway Estate streets are named after famous musicians; at the Bettws Estate the names of Rivers are used; at the Gaer, writers and poets; at St Julian's Artists; at Malpas Court, Scientists at Ringland, famous Seamen and at Somerton, Trees. So if you know your musicians, rivers, etc, you you can quite simply locate your street.

Haphazard

Such was not the case in Pill where the streets were named in a most haphazard fashion. For example, when pirates were rampant on the high seas one of their numbers, a Frenchman named Colyn Dolphyn, sailed up the Bristol Channel and captured a Newport land-owner, Sir Henry Stradling, and held him for a ransom. To secure his release Sir Harry had to sell his manors at Bassaleg and Rogerstone, Tregwilym and probably Westgate Villa. In order not to be caught napping again Sir Harry ordered a watch tower to be built to look out for the pirate. Eventually Colyn Dolphyn got his just deserts. He was attracted by the light of the watch tower; his ship was wrecked on the sands and eventually he was hanged. But his infamous memory is perpetuated by the name of Dolphin Street, off Comercial Road.

Named after Buildings and Places

Many of the Pill streets seemed to have been named after their proximity to existing buildings and places. For example, **Courtybella** was taken from a house named Cwrty Bella which is clearly shown on the 1837 ordnance sheet of the area. As time went on the name was changed to "Court-y-bella", and later the hyphens were dropped.

Dock Parade was named because of its nearness to the Docks. **Ebenezer Terrace** because of its proximity to the Ebenezer Welsh Chapel which was built in 1829 (and still exists—1983).* **Mill Parade** was named after the nearby Steam Corn Mill; **South, East** and **West Market Streets** because they surrounded the Cattle Market. **Temple Street** was named after the Baptist Temple in Commercial Road (demolished after the second world war to make way for a petrol station).

Watchhouse Parade was named after the Watch House used by the Customs Officers working at the Docks, **Commercial Road** was so

---

*Originally Ebenezer Terrace was called **Poplar Row** because of the wood of Poplar Trees planted nearby by **The Friars.**

named because it was an extension of Commercial Street and formed
the "commercial" area of Newport.

Topical Events

Other streets were named after topical events, eg **Alma**—Battle of the
River Alma in the Crimean War 1854 in which Lord Raglan took part.
Some were taken from historical names, eg **Jeddo** is the old name for
Tokyo. It was changed in 1868 at the time the streets were being named.
Coomassie—a town in Ghana destroyed in 1874 by Sir Garnet Wolseley
—probably from where **Wolseley** Street derived its name. **Wingate** Street
—Sir Francis Wingate was a British General and Governor of Sudan
from 1899-1916.

Royalty

Some streets are named after Royalty, eg **Albert, Arthur, Alexandra,
George, Charlotte** and **Alice.**

Dignitaries

Other streets appear to be named after local dignitaries, builders, etc,
Nathaniel **Daniel** was a Freeman of the Borough who died in 1877, Job
Francis was a scavenging contractor for the Newport Corporation who
died in 1904, Conyers **Kirby** was a surveyor for the Board of Health
about 1860, Pearce **Bolt** was a builder and Mayor of Newport.

Ruperra and **New Ruperra** Streets were named after Ruperra Castle
which was one of the homes of the Morgans (the family of Lord
Tredegar) who had many interests in Pill. **Mountjoy** Street gets its name
from Lord Mountjoy a nobleman who lived in the town. **Raglan** Street
after Lord Raglan, **Brunel** Street after Isambard Kingdom Brunel.

Christian Names

Other streets carry Christian names or surnames, probably those of
the contractors, builders, etc, working on the construction of the houses
and streets or those of their wives, eg. **Frederick, David, Marion,
Williams, Lewis, John.**

Mendalgief Road was original spelt 'Mendle Gief" or "Mendalgyf"
and was the site of the Manor of Mendalgief, home of the Kemeys
family.

Cork Road

Cork Road (just inside the Alexandra Dock) derives its name from
the adjoining Cork Wharf to which the ships would arrive from the City
of Cork in Southern Ireland, and discharge their cattle. It is interesting
to note that these cattle were driven through the Pill streets to New
Street where they were slaughtered behind Hockeys the Butchers (129
Commercial Road) for distribution to the rest of the Town. This
slaughterhouse was demolished early this decade to make way for flats.

Quiet Woman's Row

Another interesting name was Quiet Woman's Row—a street off Dock Parade. The origin of this name even puzzled the authorities as far back as 1897. At an Inquest that year the Coroner asked if anyone in the Court could explain its origin. A woman hailing from the District said that it was the most rowdy, ill-behaved street in Newport, containing many law-breakers, and it was beyond her understanding. A juryman enlightened the Coroner by the information that it was christened "contrariwise" by the late landlord.

Disappeared

Some of the names like **York Place, Globe Cottages, Wedlakes Court, Speedwell Street, Ship Lane** and **Garden Lane** disappeared some time ago. Other streets have changed their names—**Alexandra Road** was once called Inkerman Street, and **St Michael Street,** High Street.

Redevelopment

Since the redevelopment many streets have disappeared but the Council has retained some names by calling the new Estates with the old names, eg **Kirby, Daniel, Francis, Williams, Herbert, Charlotte** and **Lewis.**

The Old Town Dock and the Alexandra Dock

Newport's First Boat

In the years 1674 and 1675 a ship was built at Newport called the "Tredegar of Newport". The total cost was £604 whereof John Morgan of Tredegar contributed £452, the blockmaker, sailmaker, ropemaker, plumber and cooper contributing the work and material to the amount of the remaining £152. This was the first ship built at Newport.

The "Tredegar of Newport" sailed to the West Indies and in 1676 made a voyage from Barbados bringing back the following cargo:—

> 78 butts (casks of beer or wine); 3 puncheons (large casks of rum, beer or wine); 99 hogsheads (large casks of beer or cider); 14 barrels of sugar; 136 bags of ginger and 16 bags of cotton.

The Captain's name was William Wravall.

Early Shipping

One of the earliest records of shipping in Newport indicates that in 1791 over two hundred vessels called at the Port and nearly two hundred and fifty left, the only export at that time being coal. These vessels discharged and loaded their cargoes at the many wharfs on the river bank from the Castle to where now stands the Alexandra Dock.

"Floating Dock" proposed

As the years went by it became obvious that the wharfs could not cope with the vast increase in trade. By 1795 the number of ships calling at the wharfs had increased by 50%, but it was not until the turn of the century that serious thought was given to the construction of a Dock. The idea was first seriously entertained in 1831 when the cost was estimated at £60,000. Whether it was the cost which made the promoters hesitate is not clear, but it was not until 1835 that a meeting of all interested parties was held at the King's Head Hotel. From that time things moved quickly and by the end of the year the Newport Docks Bill had passed all its stages through Parliament and a two year contract was granted to Messrs Dike and Meyrick of Bristol.

The Start

Work commenced on the 5 December 1835. At the opening ceremony several hundred people had gathered to await the Mayor who arrived at 12.15 pm accompanied by R J Blewitt Esq of Llantarnam Abbey and several other wealthy inhabitants. Having taken off his coat, the Mayor cut some turf to the deafening shouts of the crowd who eagerly awaited the opening of the several barrels of Castle Brewery **XXX** beer which was liberally distributed amongst them. (About 1821 Newport Castle was converted to a Brewery—hence the name of the beer.)

Slow Progress

The 1831 estimate of £60,000 had now risen to £200,000 and because of strikes, hold-ups caused by the difficult nature of the work, and the lack of capital, instead of taking two years to complete the project it took seven.

"The Infant Liverpool"

However, on the 10 October 1842 the New Town Dock opened and Newport was called "The Infant Liverpool". Some estimates say that the total cost was slightly less than £200,000 but others put it nearer £300,000. Whatever the cost the residents of Pillgwenlly were proud to have this outstanding feat of engineering within its boundaries. Fine ships of some 1,200 tons with sails set and yards manned floated through the Dock with the greatest of ease.

Extension Necessary

For more than a decade trade increased by leaps and bounds—the New Town Dock was nearly always full, and at times it was possible to walk from one side to the other stepping from ship to ship. By 1854 it was evident that an extension was a pressing necessity and Parliamentary approval was obtained. By 1858 the extension was complete and on 1st March of that year the extended Town Dock was opened with much festivity. A lengthy procession consisting of the Police, the Army, Civic Dignitaries, many bands, 3,000 Sunday School Scholars, etc, wound its way through the Town to the Dock where the opening ceremony was performed.

Special medals were struck, a Ball was held in the Town Hall, and extra trains were laid on to bring people from the Valleys to see the fireworks and the illuminations. (The illuminations were gas, of course, and on the 2 March were blown out by a gale, only to be re-lit and enjoyed later in the week.)

The Town Dock closes

For many years the Town Dock enjoyed much prosperity and provided much needed work for the people of Newport and Pillgwenlly, and now instead of "The Infant Liverpool" was called "The Second Liverpool". With the opening of the Alexandra Dock in 1875 the need for the Town Dock diminished. In 1884 the two Docks were amalgamated and in 1929 the Town Dock closed to be filled in three years later.

The Alexandra Dock

In 1865 it was realised that the extended Town Dock would not be able to cater for the rapidly improving trade of Newport and the Alexandra Dock Company was formed to formulate proposals for a larger Dock further south. By the 28 May 1866 the necessary approvals had been obtained, and on that day Lady Tredegar (his Lordship was Chairman of the Company) cut the first sod on what we know today to be the Alexandra North Dock.

The contract, worth more than a half a million pounds, was given to Messrs Griffiths and Thomas and it was nearly seven years before the work was completed.

The Alexandra North Dock opens

The opening ceremony was carried out with great enthusiasm on the 13 April 1875, by the Mayoress (Mrs Benjamin Evans) in the unavoidable absence of Lady Tredegar. A public breakfast took place in the Victoria Hall, Bridge Street, and in the evening the town was brilliantly illuminated.

The South Dock opens

So rapidly did the shipments increase following the opening of the North Dock that as the nineteenth century closed, plans were already being made for the construction of another Dock further south and by 1907 the South Dock was completed. Access to this Dock was directly from the Bristol Channel, and it was on the 14 July 1914 that HRH Prince Arthur of Connaught opened what was at that time the largest Sea Lock Entrance in the world which gave access not only to the South Dock but from there to the North Dock.

Prosperity Remains

The coal trade, on which the Port was founded has now ceased, and its place taken by other bulk cargoes and a wide range of general cargo both exports and imports. The Docks brought prosperity not only to Pillgwenlly but to Newport generally, and is still ranked amongst one of the busiest Ports in the country.

Some Well Known Personalities

Peter Wright
—Seaman, Councillor, Mayor, Sportsman and Champion Wrestler

Seaman

Peter Wright, born in 1867 at Grangemouth on the Firth of Forth, spent most of his early life at sea and it was not until he reached the age of 32 that he arrived in Pill as a Contractor in connection with shipping in the Port.

Athlete of Renown

Although a great orator, a fine Councillor and a champion of the less privileged, perhaps his best qualities were to be found in the field of sport. He was an athlete of renown, and much of what he gained from his successes went to charities. In 1882 he vanquished all competitors in the one mile swimming championship in the Firth of Forth and also won the competition for throwing the discus. Abroad, equally as at home, he gained renown for his prowess in athletic competitions as, for instance in 1889, when he won the five mile race of Calcutta and the 120 yards hurdles and long jump.

Champion Wrestler

But of all the sports at which he excelled wrestling was his greatest love from the early age of thirteen, when he learned the art from his father. He held the heavyweight championship of Wales, the middleweight championship of the United Kingdom, and wrestled amongst the world champions, giving most of his prize money to charities. Unselfishly he taught the art of wrestling to the less privileged, establishing a physical culture class for newsboys and becoming Hon Instructor to the Constables of the Borough and the County. He organised many wrestling events for charity using the Pill Harriers Grounds on a number of occasions.

Councillor and Mayor

Peter Wright was first elected Councillor for the Alexandra Ward in 1905 and proved so popular that in 1908 when re-elected there were great scenes of enthusiasm such as never had been experienced in Pill. After the usual speeches he was bundled into a wagonette and a tour was made of the Pill Streets, led by St Michael's Drum and Fife Band! He remained a Councillor for a number of years and in 1919-20 was elected Mayor of the Town, when, rather than have a Mayoral Dinner, he gave the money towards the war widows of the Town. He was a great public speaker having a remarkably steady voice and a deliberate style of delivery which compelled a wrapt attention on the part of his audience. He was the first Labour Councillor to be made an Alderman.

Benefactor

Councillor Wright was a man of many talents, a striking personality who would not only wrestle with opponents in the ring, but with the many social problems of his day. He was an ardent Socialist, a life long abstainer, a generous benefactor, an excellent orator, an outstanding sportsman and a tireless worker who did much for his fellow men and women during his lifetime.

W H Davies
—Famous Poet, Prose Writer and Super Tramp

Unique Works

The town of Newport cannot boast many fine writers, but in W H Davies, Pillgwenlly can boast of an author whose unique works are read throughout the whole of the English speaking world. A man whose name is included amongst those famous giants of literature like Dickens, Masefield and Tennyson.

Birthplace

In writing about WHD it is necessary first to put the records straight. It is popularly believed that he was born at the Church House Pub in Portland Street, and a plaque giving this information can be seen today on the wall above the entrance to these premises.

It is likely, however, that he was born (in 1871) either next door or a few doors away where he remained for four years with his father (Francis), his mother (Mary) and his backward brother (Frank). When WHD was three his father died, soon after the birth of his sister Matilda, and when the mother re-married the three children went to live with the grandfather, Captain Francis Davies who at that time had retired from the sea and was lincensee of the Church House Pub (1875).

Christian Grandmother

In 1879 when WHD was eight his grandfather gave up the pub and moved (with WHD's grandmother—Lydia) to 38 Raglan Street. Lydia, who was a mature Christian and a member of the Commercial Road Baptist Church, tried to bring her grandson up in the Christian tradition, and tried to interest him in such books as the Bible, Paradise Lost and Pilgrim's Progress. To some degree she succeeded, for in his younger days it is believed that he professed Christianity and was baptised by the Rev Evan Thomas the Pastor of Commercial Road Baptist Church. He became a member of the Band of Hope and is reputed to have read a paper before the Mutual Improvement Society at the Church.

In 1883 when he was twelve WHD and the family moved to 21 Upper Lewis Street.

Education

WHD's early education took place at the Trinity Boys' School in Temple Street and probably at the mixed Trinity School in Church Street—both schools run mainly by the Holy Trinity Church in Potter Street.

When the Alexandra School opened in 1883 the first headmaster (Richard Davies) was a friend of Lydia and a leading member of the Commercial Road Baptist Church. So, believing that the new headmaster's influence would help her grandson, she quickly changed schools.

Pilfering

But neither his headmaster nor his grandmother had much influence on the strong-willed WHD who not only played truant from school, and had frequent fights with his friends, but soon took to petty pilfering in the Pillgwenlly shops. He was either leader or deputy leader of a wild gang and for his misconduct was given a number of strokes of the birch.

Wanderlust

Unlike his contemporaries, the restless WHD could not settle to a steady job and by the time he was twenty two (1893), having learnt to drink heavily, he was off to the USA where he became a "devil-may-care" vagrant and became known as "The Super Tramp".

After five years of roaming the States he returned to Newport but he remained only twelve months before the wanderlust gripped him again, and this time at twenty eight he set off to ride (without paying) the freight trains across Canada. All went well until the 20 March 1899 when, with his friend "Three Fingered Jack", he tried to jump a fast passenger train en route to Winnipeg. WHD slipped and the moving train severed his right leg. The doctors found it necessary to amputate, and soon he was fitted with an artificial limb.

Poor

Undaunted he returned to London in the hope of settling down to become a successful author, but it was not to be. He became so poor that he could not afford a drink and at times was taken for a teetotaller.

When he was thirty one, in 1902 his poverty and his restlessness compelled him to be on the move again—this time as a Pedlar in the Midlands selling laces and pins, etc. Although he was still writing, he gave up all hope of getting his poems published.

The Break

It was not until early in 1905 that the break came. Influential writers like George Bernard Shaw encouraged him and he returned to his mother's house (6 Llanwern Street) in October to look for a place of his own where he could settle down and write. From Llanwern Street he moved to Woodland Road, and from there to Dudley Street, but was persuaded by Edward Thomas, the Welsh Poet, to leave Newport, and in 1906 went to Sevenoaks in Kent. Mr and Mrs Thomas paid his rent, and although some income was forthcoming from his writings, he was still desperately poor. Despite the fact that his annual volumes of poetry were described as lyrical masterpieces, they made him little money.

London

Before the start of the First World War WHD left Sevenoaks for London where he seems to have spent much time pursuing and conquering members of the opposite sex, and writing poems of his experiences.

By the time he was fifty two (1923) WHD was becoming tired of being a bachelor and shocked his friends and relatives by marrying Helen Payne, a shy young girl in her early twenties, who had been his mistress. Despite the differences in their ages, the marriage was a most happy one. They moved to the Cotswold village of Nailsworth to be near Newport and spent seventeen happy years there.

Death

WHD made a number of visits to Newport and was given a civic luncheon in 1930 in recognition of his work. In 1938 both he and his wife visited the town and went to Portland Street, where in the company of the Poet Laureate, John Masefield, a plaque was unveiled at the Church House. Amongst the crowd was a Mr W J Anthony who told WHD that he remembered his father and grandfather. John Masefield told the large crowd that too often poets were not regarded until they had been fifty years in their grave, and it was fitting that Newport had honoured their poet whilst he was still alive.

About this time WHD's health began to fail and in 1940 he died.

A Christian

A few years before his death WHD became a Christian and his newfound faith helped him to face death bravely. One of his best known poems contain the following words:

> "A poor life this if, full of care
> We have no time to stand and stare"

WHD had led a restless life but his death and faith brought the peace for which he had searched for sixty nine years. He now had inherited eternity to stand and stare on the face of his God whom he had learnt to love in his latter years.

Loss

Pillgwenlly had lost one of her geniuses—a man whose friends had included Jacob Epstein, the prominent sculptor, George Bernard Shaw, the brilliant Irish writer, and Walter Sickert, the distinguished painter. He was a man whose genius was compared to that of Daniel Defoe the writer of Robinson Crusoe.

WHD's death occurred in 1940 when the Nation was pre-occupied with war and possible invasion, and to a large degree went unnoticed. In the "death column" of the *Weekly Argus* dated the 5 October the following simple announcement appeared:

> "On 26 September William Henry Davies the dear brother of Alice Davies, 14 Bailey Street."

But throughout the whole of the English speaking world, the death of WHD the Tramp Poet caused regret and to the people of Pillgwenlly and Newport the loss was especially severe. Not only was he a writer of poetry of Elizabethan freshness and charm, he was also a prose writer of distinction. Considering his limited education and his early life of hardship and uncertainty, he was truly a man of outstanding capabality and a real independence of mind which was recognised by the University of Wales who had made him a Doctor of Literature.

Revolutionary

In some ways WHD was a revolutionary. Some of his poems show his anger at the unequal distribution of material possessions which allows some to live in luxury whilst others are homeless and hungry.

> "I count the tramp as noble as that man
> Who lives in idleness on wealth bequeathed."

Love of Nature

WHD's poems (published by Jonathan Cape) reveal an intimate knowledge of and love for nature. An account of his life is given in his Autobiography published in 1926 by the same firm.

Alderman Mrs Mary Ann Hart, OBE, JP
—Newport's Only Woman Freeman

Women's Lib

Women's Lib began in Newport in 1925 when Mrs Mary Hart of 67 Lewis Street was the first woman to be elected to the Council. Previously she had been made the first woman magistrate and subsequently the first woman Alderman, the first woman Mayor and the first and only woman Freeman of the Borough.

Philosopher and Guide

Mrs Hart was a philosopher and guide who worked quietly for her people, never refusing advice to anyone, no matter what political persuasion. She did most of her work, not in the Town Hall or the Civic Centre, but in 67 Lewis Street (demolished in 1976) where the door was always open to anyone requiring her help.

First and Only Woman Freeman

After having the honour of becoming Newport's first lady Mayor in 1937 she had the further honour on the 13 April 1954 of becoming Newport first female Honorary Freeman, just after she had resigned from the Council having served it for twenty nine years and reached her four score years.

It was fitting that the honour was conferred upon her by another Pill Councillor who was Mayor in that year—the late Bill Pinnell BEM of 26 Dolphin Street. As she sat in the Council Chamber, a small figure in blue with a spray of yellow roses on her breast, a number of Members paid high tribute to the work she had done for the people of Newport and especially for those living in Pill. A "titter" went around the sunlit crowded Council Chamber as the Mayor grinned broadly and put his arm affectionately around Mrs Hart and referred to her as "this great lady". The late Alderman Tyack reminded the Council that the freedom of the Borough was something conferred very infrequently on people who merit it and Mrs Hart ranked with such eminent citizens as Lord Tredegar and Field Marshall Viscount Montgomery.

Mrs Hart ended her response with the words "work hard for the Town"—something she herself had done for many years.

Mair Gwenlli

In addition to all this, in 1938, for the first time in the history of Newport, a Mayor of the Town was given an honorary degree and a Bardic Title at the Cardiff Gorsedd on the 4th August at the Cardiff Castle. She became Mair Gwenlli (Mary of Pillgwenlly) and was the first Newport citizen for a number of years to receive a Bardic Title. Born at Bridgend, she was Welsh speaking.

The Right Honourable J H Thomas
——The Pill Errand Boy who became Friend of Kings, Cabinet Minister and Nearly Prime Minister

Poverty

Jimmy Thomas was born in poor circumstances at 51 (now 74) George Street, Pill, in 1874.

It was five years later that Jimmy attended the Infants' Department of the National Schools opposite St Paul's Church in Commercial Street—a school founded in 1840 by Sir Charles Morgan which, during its lifetime of fifty seven years, educated many notable people including five Mayors of the Town. For a penny Jimmy would be entitled to a week's education, but later when he was elevated to the senior school the fees doubled. He was not a strong boy, and, as he could not win an argument by fighting was compelled to use his eloquence, and so the force of brilliance of expression was born.

To help eke out the family budget when he was seven, Jimmy found it necessary to start work, and while continuing his education, he found himself a job in Phillips little Chemist's shop tucked between the National Schools and the King William IV Public House in Commercial Street. Five years later he left school and found employment with the High Street Drapers "Baker & Manhire". At fourteen he joined the Great Western Railway as a "call-boy" and soon became a cleaner earning 7/- per week. He was later promoted to Fireman and Engine Driver.

Politics

When he was twenty he became interested in politics and a year later publicly expressed his views in political meetings in the Town. He soon became an active member of the Trades Union Council in Newport, and it was his sincere belief in the right of every man, no matter what his environment or circumstances, to have a fair chance of making the world better for having lived in it. It was not equality he wanted but equality of opportunity.

It was not long before Jimmy Thomas was transferred by the Great Western Railway to Swindon. He insisted that this move was brought about by his political activities. His move, however, in no way inhibited his political life, for in 1919 he was invited to stand for Parliament by the Cardiff Labour Party. He refused this invitation in favour of the Derby Constituency—a seat which he won in 1910 and held until his resignation in 1936. During his campaign he was so impoverished after putting what money he had into the "fighting fund", that he had to borrow £5 to pay his expenses home for Christmas.

Freedom of the Borough and Cabinet Minister

In 1924 he was made an Honorary Freeman of the Borough and in the same year when Mr Ramsay McDonald, the Prime Minister, formed his Cabinet, J H Thomas was included as the Secretary of State for the Colonies. In 1929 he became Lord Privy Seal and Minister of Employment; in 1930 he was Secretary of State for the Dominions, retaining his office in the National Government of 1931. In 1935 he became Colonial Secretary In addition he was a Privy Counsellor. He held Cabinet Office until 1936 when, as a member of Baldwin's National Government, at budget time, he was accused of betraying Government secrets, and although he denied deliberately making these disclosures, he resigned. So his career, in which he made friends of kings, world ranking politicians and leading people in all walks of life, ended on a sad note.

Proud of the Constitution

In March 1924 he visited his home town with the Duke of York and as he passed "Baker & Manhire" he saw, standing at the entrance to the draper's shop the same Manager who had appointed him as an errand boy forty years ago. Then on to St Paul's Church where he had attended Sunday School; across the road the National Schools where he had paid for and received his education; next door was still the brass plate of Phillips the Chemist which he had cleaned forty odd years ago. Then on to Pill—to George Street where he was born. That night he spoke in the Central Hall opposite Palmyra Place and said with great eloquence and emotion:

"I am proud of the Constitution which enables me to stand on this platform within fifty yards of where I was an errand boy and forty yards from where I received my education—to come back to my Town, to my people, to my old mates, to my comrades whilst I am entrusted with one fourth of the Globe. I am proud of a Constitution which enables an Engine Cleaner of today to be a Prime Minister of tomorrow."

Retirement and Death

In 1946 Jimmy Thomas returned to South Wales and lived with his wife (a Pill girl whom he married in 1898) until his death in January 1949.

Had it not been for the alleged indiscretion in 1936, Pill might have been able to boast of a Prime Minister who was a man of extrordinary talent and energy.

Tom (Toyer) Lewis
—Pill's Boy Hero

Docks Tragedy

On the 2 July 1909 work was proceeding steadily on the Docks Extension and workmen had almost completed the framework of the two 200′ trenches so that the concrete could be poured between the timbers, which, when set would make the walls of the new Lock. Seventy nine men were quickly coming towards the end of a hard day's work when suddenly at 5.20 pm the whole of one trench collapsed killing and trapping many of the men working below.

At 7.30 that evening, Tom (Toyer) Lewis of Wallis Street, a boy who sold Arguses to make a few pence to supplement the family income, went to the Docks and there witnessed the dead bodies being brought up and taken to the mortuary; the injured being rushed off to hospital, or the Workhouse Hospital as it was then called. But half the men were still trapped below the timbers, some dead—a few alive.

Little Tom's Bravery

At 11.30 pm Tom heard the workmen asking for someone to go down into the trench through the collapsed timbers to attempt to free some of the trapped men who could be heard groaning below. They looked around for a small brave man to tackle the hazardous task of squeezing through the closely collapsed timbers, but no-one small enough was to be found. "What about me?" said little Tom much to the amazement of the experienced navvies and officials standing by. After some consultation Tom's offer was accepted and preparations were made for his perilous descent. As he descended down the trench squeezing his thin body through the tangled timbers he saw a navvy lying on his face—dead. Through the muddy twisted timbers his eyes caught sight of a lad named King who was too severely trapped for Tom to attempt release. Lying on his back near the lad was a man with heavy timbers lying across his arms and legs. With hammer and chisel Tom first released his arms, keeping the man's spirits up by supplying him with brandy sent down by a rope from the dockside fifty feet up. Once the arms were released Tom continued to work amongst the creaking timbers on the man's legs. After two and a half hours one leg was released and as Tom started to work on the second leg, the timbers began to move once again. The men at the top insisted that Tom came up and reluctantly he had to leave the trapped man or chance being buried alive. The straining and grinding of the timbers continued—the waters rushed in—the lad King disappeared in the flood. Miraculously the man who Tom had partially freed was saved and pulled up the following morning.

Civilian VC

For his valiant efforts Tom (Toyer) Lewis received the following message from the King and Queen:

"Their Majesties are anxious to express to the boy Lewis their admiration of the heroism which he displayed, and their congratulations on his wonderful escape."

Later Tom received the Civilian VC—the Albert Medal which, towards the end of the year he received from the King at Buckingham Palace.

Argus Fund

No time was lost by the *South Wales Argus* for their "Argus Boy" in starting a fund to reward Tom in some tangible way for his bravery. Contributions began to pour in, and soon there was enough to send him to Scotland to start an engineering apprenticeship with the firm of contractors (Easton Gibb & Son) who were the contractors for the ill-fated lock at the Docks.

So a brave Pill boy was awarded for his outstanding bravery and given a new start in life which he never expected.

<h2 style="text-align:center">Councillor Bill Moore
—Youth Leader, Councillor and Preacher</h2>

A Giant

When people in Pill talk about their YMCA they invariably mention the late Bill Moore who was its Founder and Secretary for over half a century. Bill Moore was a man with a fervent compassion to ensure that young people had a chance to learn about the true values of life both morally and spiritually, and although a man of only small stature, he was a giant as far as the community of Pill was concerned.

The Rivet Warmers' Institute

It was on the 3 March 1919 in the old Branch Police Station in Temple Street that Mr Moore, in his twenties, started a recreational club club for the rivet warmers working at the Alexandra Docks. It was intended to be for boys only, but was so popular that it attracted men and boys between 14 and 60 and some were the toughest in the District. This Club was soon to become the Pillgwenlly YMCA and became so prosperous that in 1955 a large sports ground was opened in Mendalgief Road at a cost of £16,000, much of which Mr Moore was instrumental in raising.

Money Raising Events

Money was raised in every conceivable way, but the most popular event was probably "the 6d Hop" when hundreds danced to the music of the Pill YMCA Jazz Band each Saturday night.

Mr Moore would organise special fund raising events, and one such event was an open air boxing tournament on what Pill people know as "the ballast" off Mendalgief Road. Top of the bill was the famous Jimmy Wilde—a great friend of Mr Moore with whom he had worked in the coal pits of his youth. He showed a great interest in sport and for a number of years was the Organiser of the Welsh Baseball Association and the Monmouthshire Baseball League.

Many Interests

Bill Moore was a man with unlimited energy for in addition to his work for the YMCA, he was a local lay preacher for over fifty years, a Councillor, Pastor of the East Usk Road Baptist Church for fifteen and a half years, as well as having a full time job as Clerk to the Newport and East Mon Hospitals Management Committee.

Fire Station

When in 1960 the disused Fire Station near the YMCA Sports Ground became available, Mr Moore was again instrumental in its purchase and adaptation for a new YMCA Headquarters, and where it remains today as a memorial to one of Pill's most loveable characters.

Autobiography

In his later years, Mr Moore spent some time writing his auto-biography, but death came before he could finish it. In that autobiography there is much good advice which perhaps could be summed up in one quotation—"Give to the world the best you can and the best will come back to you." Bill Moore did just that.

Sport

Jerry Shea
—a Brilliant Rugby Player—All-Round Athlete—a Gentleman

National Hero of Wales

Jerry Shea, one of the most colourful personalities ever to figure in Welsh Sport was once described in the London Press as the National Hero of Wales. In the years following the 1914-18 war, he played rugby for Wales as well as gaining a remarkable reputation as a first class boxer and track athlete. One of the most brilliant centre threequarters ever produced by Pill Harriers and Newport, he was largely responsible for some of the successful seasons of both Clubs, particularly the Pill Harriers invincible team of 1918-19.

Wales and Wigan

Playing for Wales against England at Swansea in 1920 he performed the amazing scoring feat, being personally responsible for sixteen of the nineteen points registered by Wales.

Later he became a professional for Wigan (signing for that Club for what was at that time a record fee) and played for three seasons captaining Wigan for the last two. At no time, however, did he make his home in the North, and a few years later decided to return to the Principality and helped to form a professional rugby team at Pontypridd. This team played for two years and then disbanded.

Boxing Fame

He was almost equally well known in the boxing world. Standing 5′6″ and weighing under 10 stone 7 lbs he quickly rose to prominence in the welterweight class by his remarkable hitting power.

He was victorious over many top class boxers and it was most appropriate that his boxing career should end with a fight against Johnny Basham at Newport—both men friends in private life made their last appearance in the ring together.

Athlete and Swimmer

Jerry Shea was an accomplished athlete too, and as a regular member of Pill Harriers won the championship for 1,000 yards, but it was at 440 yards that he achieved his greatest success, winning three open professional handicaps at this distance. He was also a capable swimmer.

Highly Respected

At 33 he decided to give up his sporting activities and by this time was known by everyone in Pill and at the Docks where he worked. At the early age of 55 he died suddenly while returning by car to his home at 86 Alma Street.

Just after his death his sporting life was described as "romantic", "daring", "adventurous". As a rugby player he was great, as a man he was lovable. As you met him on the streets of Pill, the warm grip of his hand and the kindness in his voice revealed the affection which flowed out of him.

Johnny Basham
—Middleweight Champion of Europe

European Champion

Few fighters did more to further the cause of Welsh and British boxing than Pill newspaper boy Johnny Basham who was middleweight champion of Europe and welterweight champion of Great Britain from 1914-20. He was an outright winner of the Lonsdale Belt, and at his prime was probably the most polished boxer at any weight in Great Britain.

A Generous Man

Johnny was a very generous man and during his lifetime won and lost a fortune. By 1947 he was in poor circumstances and in June of that year the Newport Sportsman's Committee had arranged to give him a helping hand by organising a testimonial tournament. It was planned to raise sufficient funds to provide him with a life pension in recognition of the distinction he gave to Wales and Newport in the boxing world.

However, it was a pension that he was never to receive for on Saturday morning the 7 June, Johnny collapsed and died at his home, 12 Mountjoy Place, aged 57.

Lonsdale Belt

Johnny's Lonsdale Belt was in the possession of Pill Boxing Promoter, the late Joe Carr for some time, but was sold at Christies (London) in March 1954.

118

Pill Harriers

An article in the *South Wales Argus* on the 1 September 1892 begins "The Pillgwenlly Athletic Club is at present an organisation ranked among the juniors, but it has at its head several gentlemen who are determined to make for it a name, and before many seasons are over they expect to turn out fine teams in all departments."

The Reporter who wrote this can be ranked amongst the prophets, for what he said certainly became true, and although the history of the Club was interrupted for a number of years, they have come back, and are once again ranked amongst the finest Junior Clubs in South Wales.

It is not generally known that the Club was formed in 1882 by the Assistants at the Liverpool House—an establishment on the corner of Commercial Road and Potter Street described as Universal Outfitters and Mercantile Company. (The building remains today.) It is said that the young men of Pill would "hang around" the building, and to keep them out of mischief the Proprietors of Liverpool House would encourage them in sporting activities by donating sports equipment and generally help them to play games.

The first game to be played by Pill Harriers was cricket, and their first ground was at Penmain Wharf off Church Street. After a successful cricket season it was decided to form a Football Section, and in their first season they reached the semi-final of the Newport Challenge Cup, but the Club, then called Liverpool House Rovers, suffered defeat at the hands of Newport Blue Stars.

Encouraged by their achievements on the football field, in 1891 it was thought advisable to have a more convenient ground. At this time Pill had been experiencing its first immigrants—the navvies who had come over from Ireland to help fill in the "Marshes". One of their pastimes was the game called hurling (the Irish form of hockey), and in pursuit of this sport they had prepared a piece of land belonging to the Alexandra Dock Company off Mendalgief Road. The Irishmen's work in preparing this land eventually benefited the Liverpool House Rovers who were able to lease from the Dock Company a ready-made rugby ground far superior to any in South Wales at that time. The ground which was opened in 1893, provided, in addition to football, cricket and a cycle track.

The *South Wales Argus* reported "There is evidently no lack of enterprise down Pill way. When completed the ground will be one of the driest and most complete belonging to any Junior Organisation in the Country."

After winning the Newport Challenge Cup, it was decided that the teams to be met in 1892 should be "of better class" and the fixture list for that year included such teams as Abergavenny, Pontymister, Pontypridd, Morriston, Stroud, Swindon, and Newport Seconds.

Not content with rugby and cricket, the Club took on the popular game of baseball, and its membership soon increased to almost two hundred.

By the turn of the century the Club was in a most healthy state, and enjoyed many years of prosperity until the outbreak of war in 1939 when the ground was taken over for industrial purposes. At the end of hostilities a further prosperous period was anticipated, as at the outbreak of war negotiations were proceeding for the acquisition of a new sports ground, but when the end of the war came (1945) it was found that the ground was not available.

So on the 3 June 1947 the Chairman of the Club (Mr J B Pitchford) had the painful duty of proposing that the Club be wound up and "that the £116 credit be given to the Newport Athletic Club in acknowledgement of their loyalty and friendship in the past."

Despite the fact that Pill Harriers went out of being, rugby still continued to be played in Pill by such teams as the Hibernians and Pill Labour Hall, and it was the amalgamation of these two teams in the 1978-79 Season which brought about the formation of the new Pill Harriers. Their first season was so successful that they found themselves in four cup finals, and although they only won one, all were closely fought. Although the Club had no home pitch, and no permanent HQ in Pill they gradually consolidated their position, and in recent years have found a home pitch not far from their old ground off Mendalgief Road where the Council have demolished many old houses. A new Club House has been erected close by.

The Club is now looking forward to ending this century as it began by producing rugby players of such high calibre as to play for their Country. Pill Harriers can boast a number of Welsh Internationals, but the most famous of these are perhaps the father and son combination of George and William (Bunner) Travers. They were the outstanding father and son combination of their era, and were honoured as two of the greatest hookers Wales has ever produced. George had twenty five caps (1903-11) and William (who also played for Newport) twelve caps (1937-49). There are only four sets of fathers and sons gaining Welsh caps and Pill can proudly boast one of these.

Many personalities could be mentioned when writing about Pill Harriers, but a history would not be complete without a mention of Jim Grace who was Chairman for many years and devoted a great deal of his time to the running of the Club. Mention should also be made of the present President of the Club Fred Emms who many will remember playing for Pill and Newport just before the second world war.

Bob Edwards and Ushiro Judo Club

The Father Hill Memorial School building in Oswald Road still serves a useful purpose although no longer functioning as originally intended. Occupying the ground floor is the Ushiro Judo Club which was formed in Ringland in 1975, by Bob Edwards (2nd Dan), the Englishman who loves Wales. For seventeen years he has lived in Newport, marrying Janice and raising his two sons. Wayne is now twelve years old and John is fourteen. Both are staunch members of the Ushiro Club along with 45 Seniors and 27 Juniors.

In 1974 when he was thirtyone years old, Chatham-born Bob Edwards started his own Judo career, at what is regarded as a 'late stage'. In 1983 he can claim to have trained hundreds of youngsters, 27 of whom have had the honour of representing Wales in International Contests. For six months in 1981 he served as National Youth Judo Coach (Welsh Junior Squad). This Ushirojudokwai is an example of the 'do-it-yourself' spirit prevalent in the Pillgwenlly area. The Club has not enjoyed any grants or outside financial help although assistance from any source would be welcome. Subscriptions from members pay for equipment and rent of premises. Each year at least ten members have gained places on the Welsh Squad and 29 members have represented Gwent. More than 500 medals and trophies have been won. Active helpers in the management of this Club are Dora and John McDonnell whose son Heath is a member. Players who have been advisers to Bob Edwards are Terry Edmunds (5th Dan and recently retired police officer) and Dave Ball (2nd Dan). Another Pillgwenlly-based organisation which is performing a useful and valuable community service for the youngsters in and around the district.

(His oldest pupil, in his 50's wrote a booklet of verses to help raise finances for the Ushirokwai: JUDO MOTION IN POETRY by F E A Yates (1981) published by Starling Press of Risca.)

Carnivals and Festivals, 1974-76

Small Beginnings

For nearly ten years Pill has held its own Carnivals and Festivals when, in August of each year everyone "lets their hair down" and has a jolly good time. It all began in 1970 when the Pill Children's Playground Association held a one-day Children's Festival on the Mendalgief Recreation Ground ("The Rec") which, after running for four consecutive years was so successful that, in 1974, the newly-formed Pill Community Group, under the Chairmanship of George Bullock, decided it was time that the event should be extended to include everyone in Pill. On the foundation of the Children's Festival they built a Festival Queen, a day of street parties, a Carnival Parade, with a host of fringe activities like five-a-side soccer, tug-o'-war, shop window dressing, fun fairs, stalls, etc.

The First Carnival and Festival

So in August 1974 memories of VE Day were revived when the Pill streets were gaily decorated and eighteen street parties were held on Thursday the 22nd. Danter's Fun Fair appeared in Albion Street and various activities and competitions were going on all over Pill. On the August Monday the Carnival was the highlight of the whole Festival—thirty floats took part—thousands flocked into Pill—the local MP (Mr Roy Hughes) and the Mayor (Councillor John Marsh—a Pill Councillor) mingled with the crowds whilst the Pill residents renewed friendships with the thousands of visitors. The first full-scale Carnival and Festival was a great success and the unanimous verdict was that it must continue.

An Established Event

And so, the Carnival and Festival became an annual event, and although it must be said that none has surpassed the 1974 occasion, the people of Pill still love their own get together each August and have, albeit not without difficulty, been able to hold it regularly since 1974.

Pill Branch Library, Temple Street

The First Library in Newport
It was in 1711 that the first library was set up in Newport by the Society for the Promotion of Christian Knowledge. It consisted of 72 volumes about Anglican Divinity printed in London in the 17th and 18th centuries. The library had previously belonged to St Woolos Church founded about 530 AD by Gwynllyw father of St Cadoc.

Newport Book Club
The second library was an elite one comprising of about thirty members drawn from the gentry and professional classes able to afford the £1 annual subscription which was a lot of money in 1833.

The Mechanics Institution Library
The first library for all classes of people was set up in 1841 by the Mechanics Institute (in 1848) to become known as the Athenaeum and Mechanics Institute. It started with a mere 11 volumes and a reading room with 9 newspapers and 11 periodicals. Over the years there was a steady increase in the bookstock and by 1865 the library boasted some 14,000 volumes.

It was this library that opened the first Reading Room in Pill in 1864 at 139 Commercial Road, but owing to poor support and lack of finance, it closed in 1867.

By 1870 the A & M was in dire financial difficulties and was taken over by the Council in that year.

Branch Reading Room, 70 Commercial Road
In 1873 a second attempt to encourage the residents of Pill to read when a Reading Room was opened at 70 Commercial Road and attracted 300 residents daily and remained open until the new Reading Room was available in Temple Street on the 1 January 1890.

Temple Street Reading Room and Library
It was Lord Tredegar's generosity which enabled this building to be established in Temple Street. In 1887 it was stated that two cottages in Temple Street had been acquired and a new Reading Room for the residents of Pillgwenlly would be erected in their place. The building was erected at a cost of £1,450 and opened on the 1 January 1890. The magazine room and news room occupied the ground floor, with school rooms on the first floor.

In 1899 discussions took place about the possibility of creating a

Lending Library in Temple Street by using the first floor school rooms, but nothing came of it.

Children's Lending Library
Pillgwenlly had to wait until 1929 before it got its first Lending Library and this was for children only—the first Children's Department to be opened in Newport. It was on the 16 May 1929 that His Worship the Mayor (Councillor Walter J Griffiths JP) opened the building which was stocked with over 3,000 books which were borrowed by some 700 Pill children.

Story Hours
Story hours was one of the features of the Pill work when on alternative Saturday mornings about thirty children would gather at the library and be told a story. The story tellers were many and included some well known Newportonians like Rev D J Thomas (Minister of the Commercial Road Baptist Church), Councillor Mrs C M Lewcock, Mr and Mrs Kyrle Fletcher, Mr W. A. Gunn and Mr W J Collett.

The Library Today
The library remains today and is well used by Pill residents of all ages, the adult lending library having started in 1974.

Index

Albert Hall, Ebenezer Terrace 72
Albert Hall, Particular Baptist Church 72
Albert Hall Sunday School 52
Albert Medal 115
Albert Street 102
Albion Street 122
Alder, Dr Herman 83
Alexandra Court 94
Alexandra Docks 39-48, 50, 53, 56, 59, 80, 94, 104-106, 114, 116, 117
Alexandra Pottery 57
Alexandra Road 59, 68, 84, 94, 102, 103
Alexandra Road Baptist Church 71, 73, 75, 76
Alexandra School 92, 109
Alexandra Theatre 40
Alice Dry Dock 49
Alice Street 102
Alma Street 43, 45, 51, 72, 93, 102, 118
Alma Street Baptist Church 41, 52, 53, 72-74, 76, 86
Alma Street Mission 76
Allsopp, Rev B J 73, 74
Arnodin, F 98
Arr, Rev Wallace 73
Arthur Street 102
Atkinson, Rev 80

Bagg, Agnes 80
Bailey, Rev Fr 79
Baker and Manhire 113, 114
Baldwin Street 54, 57, 95
Baldwin Street Mission 71, 76
Ballast 55
Band of Hope 29, 31, 34, 36, 71, 81, 108
Baptist Mission Hall 83
Barfield, Rev 69
Barnes, Rev 79

Barracks, Mill Parade 12-14, 63
"Basham's" Chapel 77, 78
Basham, Johnny 118
Bates, Cyril 92
Beaufort Wharf 96
Beavon, Thomas 63
Beddis, John 76
Beer Houses 17-19, 21, 22, 28, 33, 36, 39, 46, 49
Belle Vue Lane 55, 87
Belle Vue Park 87, 88
Belle Vue School 92
Benneth, Rev John 74
Bennett, E H 93
Bethel Temple 66
Bethesda Brethren 75
Bible Christian Church 20, 65, 66
Blackburn, Ald W M 68
Blewitt, R J 104
"Bogies" 97
Bold, Rev W 78
Bolt Street 58, 102
Bolt Street School 92
Brunel Street 102
Bullock, George 122
Burris, Rev Fr 79
Bus Service 60
Bush, Miss 90
Butt, Mr 90

Calvinistic Methodism 61
Canal 9, 11, 26, 55, 57, 94
Canal Parade 13, 72
Canning, Ald 99
Capel Street 46
Cardiff Road 9, 55, 56, 87, 94, 95
Carnivals and Festivals 122
Cashmore, John, Ltd 60
Castle Street 45
Cattle Market 13-16, 18, 19, 21, 22, 24-26, 28, 33, 39, 42, 43, 45, 50, 55-57, 68, 70, 72, 85, 86, 88
Central Hall 114

Chack (Builder) 83
Charlotte Street 46, 102
Children's Lending Library 124
Childs, Rt Rev 68
Cholera 10, 15, 20, 41
Christians' Meeting Room 75
Churches and Other Religions 61-84
Church House 108
Church Street 11, 22, 56, 58, 91, 119
Cleppa Park 86
Clytha Crescent 55
Clytha Square 55, 95
Cloake, John 76
Commercial Road 9, 14, 22, 23, 55, 56, 58, 59, 90, 95, 101, 123
Commercial Road Baptist Church 35, 37, 38, 69-72, 74, 75, 85, 108
Commercial Rd Wesleyan Church 10, 19, 63, 64, 77
Coomassie Street 102
Cork Road 102
Cork Wharf 96, 102
Cornwall, Rev Alan 67
Coronation Park 87
Courtybella Farm 9, 10, 12
Courtybella Street 95
Courtybella Terrace 56, 101
Cross Street 22, 92

Dando, Rev Eric 66
Daniel Street 102
David Street 102
Davies, Ben (Water Seller) 94
Davies Coun Edward 80
Davies, Ald H J 55, 87, 88
Davies, Richard 109
Davies, Rev Fr 79
Davies, W H (Tramp Poet) 47, 91, 108-111
Defoe, Daniel 111
Dock Parade 12, 19, 56, 101, 103
Dock Street 58

Dolphin Street Mission 71
Dolphyn, Colin 101
Downes, Rev Frank 72
Druiff, Jacob 83

Ealy, Rev 79
Early Transport 58-60
East Market Street 101
East Usk Rd Baptist Church 116
Easton Gibb & Son 115
Ebbw River 22, 55
Ebenezer Welsh Calvinistic Church 9, 15, 61-63, 65, 101
Ebenezer Terrace 9, 55, 101
Edwards, Bob 120
Edwards, Rev Ebenezer 70
Electric Tramways 59
Elliott Home for Seamen 80
Elliott, Rev Edward 74
Elliott, Sir George, MP 80
Emlyn Street 92
Emmanuel Evangelical Church 72-74
Emms, Fred 120
Epstein, Joseph 111
Essery, Jim 76
Evans, Ald William 88, 94
Evans, Mrs Benjamin 106
Evans, Rev Christmas 62
Evans, Rev George 71
Evans, Rev T Emlyn 63

Family Care Housing Association 68
Father Hill Memorial School 79, 92, 120
Fausti-de-Rienzi 98
Feltham, Rev Keith 76
Festivals 122
Fevez, Rev Fr 79
Field, Rev Douglas 78
Fire Service 14, 15. 19, 20, 25, 31, 46, 51, 96
Ford, Stan 75

Fothergill, Thomas 56
Francis Street 83, 102
Freeman of the Borough 111, 112
Frederick Street, 58, 102
French, George 76

Garden Lane 103
"Gargoyles" 68
Garry, Rev W W 80
George Street 13, 56, 102, 112, 114
George Street Bridge 61
Gibson, Clive 76
Globe Cottages 103
Gorsedd Stones 88
Gospel Hall, Inkerman Street 71, 76
Grace, Jim 120
Griffith & Thomas 106
Guy Fawkes Night 95, 96
Gwynllw's Harbour 56

Habershon and Fawkner 77
"Halfway House" 94
Hardiman, Rev David 76
Harris, Rev Griffith 74
Harris, Howell 61
Harrison, Rev Graham 74
Hart, Ald Mrs M A 111, 112
Hassett, Rev Fr Joe 79
Hasser, Akmed 84
Haynes, R H 99
Hayward, Stan 76
Herbert, J A 92
Herbert Street 55, 93
Herring, Rev John 62
Hibernians RFC 120
High Street 79, 91, 103
Hill, Rev Fr 79, 92
Holland, Rev Fr 79
Holy Cross School 51, 53, 92
Holy Trinity Church 24-27, 35, 36, 39, 49, 57, 67, 68, 109
Homfray, Samuel 11, 22, 56, 70
Honeywill, Mrs M E 63, 94

Hope Chapel 69
Horse-drawn Omnibus Service 14, 22, 29, 58
Horse-drawn Tramways 47, 49, 51, 53, 58
Howarth, Rev David 78
Howell, Rev Morgan 62
Howell, Rev W J 76
Hughes, Roy, MP 122
Hunt, John, & Sons 67

Independent Chapel, Temple St 16
Ingram, Rev D W 73, 76
Inkerman Street 51, 71, 76, 103
Irish Famine 78
Irish Immigrants 9, 16, 18-20, 25

Jacks Pill 9, 13, 15, 20, 23, 26
Jeddo Street 54, 57, 95, 102
Jeffrey, Rev W 66
Jewish Synagoge—see Synagogue
John Strett 102
Jones, Ald 99
Jones, Rev H Luther 74
Jones, Rev J Meredith 74
Jones, Rev Roy 72
Jones, W M (Builder) 70
Junior Temperance Society 91

Kings Hill Well 94
Kings Parade 96
King Street 72
Kirby Street 102
Knight, Coun Les 100

Langdon, Mr 67
Lascelles, Rowley 56
Latch, Joseph 10, 15, 51
Lawrence, B (Architect) 83
Lewis Street 22, 45, 57, 83, 102, 111, 112
Lewis, Rev W Price 72
Lewis, Tom (Toyer) 114, 115

Library, Temple Street 123, 124
Lime Street 50, 57, 76, 95
Lime Street Mission 71
Liscombe, Coun John 81
Liverpool House 119
Lonsdale Belt 118

Mahoney, James, Ltd 20
Mair Gwenlly 112
Manley, Alan 76
Mariners Chapel 9, 13, 18, 20, 21, 36, 42, 46, 61, 82
Mariners Friendly Society 82
Marion Street 57, 102
Marsh, Coun John 122
Masefield, John 110
Masonic Hall, 23, 28, 32
Matthews, Rev A A 81
Mawson, T H 88
McGuinn, Dr (Councillor) 99
Meaker, Solomon 94
Mendalgief Road 55-57, 94, 102, 116, 119
Mill Parade 94
Mission to Seamen 82
Mitchell & Butlers 93
Molyneux, Rev 80
Montgomery, Lord 112
Moore (Builder) 69
Moore, Coun Bill 115, 116
Morgan, Sir Charles 9, 11, 16, 32, 56, 85, 112
Morgan, Wm (Chemist) 67
Morgan, Wm (Headmaster) 90
Morris, Rev T 65
Mosques 84
Mountjoy Gospel Hall 59, 74, 75
Mountjoy Place, 55, 118
Mountjoy Street 59, 75, 102
Muslims 84

National Eisteddfod—see Welsh National Eisteddfod

National Schools 112, 114
National Training Schools Scheme 90, 91
Navvies Mission 82, 83
Newman, Miss 90
Newport's First Boat 104
New Ruperra Street 81, 102
New Street 57, 102
New Testament Church of God 65-67
Northcotte, John 70, 74
Nowell, Jeff 73
Nowell, Joe 73, 76

O'Brien, Wm 66
Oddfellows Hall 54
Old Red Cow PH 13
Old Town Dock—see Town Dock
Ollivant, Rt Rev 67
Open Air Market 86
Orphans Friends School 23, 31, 34, 38
Osborne, B 75
Oswald Road 79, 92, 120

Parry, James 69
Parry, Wm 95
Pawnbroking 35
Penmain Wharf 119
Penny Readings 39, 42, 43
Perkins Shipyard 10
Phillips, Coun Clifford 85
Phillips, Fred (Mayor 1894) 88
Pillgwenlly—Origin of Name 86, 95
Pillgwenlly Baptist Church—see Commercial Rd Baptist Church
Pillgwenlly Branch Library 123, 124
Pillgwenlly Children's Missionary Association 91
Pill Children's Playground Association 122
Pill Gates 10, 56

Pill Harriers 117, 118
Pill Harriers' Grounds 107
Pill Labour RFC 120
Pill Park 87
Pill Road—*see* Commercial Road
Pill Well 94
Pinnell, Ald Bill 112
Police 10-13, 17, 19, 23, 24, 26, 46, 51, 96
Police Station, Temple Street, 32, 116
Poplar Row 101
Portland Street 22, 69, 70, 74, 83, 108, 110
Portland Street Methodist Church 25, 68, 69
Potter Street 56, 67, 83
Pottery Terrace 77, 92
Price (Builder) 77, 92
Price Street 54, 77, 95
Price Street Methodist Church 64, 77, 78
Prince Arthur of Connaught 106
Pring, Mrs Annie 72
Prostitution 21, 29, 33, 34, 38, 40, 43, 46, 53

Quiet Womans Row 103

"Ragged" Schools 38, 41, 43, 44, 47, 53
Raglan Street 43, 102, 108
Reading Room, Temple Street 123
"Recollections" 94-96
Redhouse Farm 57
Rees, Daniel 70
Richards, Wm 74
Ritterbert, Rev 83
Rivet Warmers Institute 116
Roman Catholic Voluntary School 91
Round Table Field 88
Ruperra Street 23, 56, 58, 84, 94, '02

Rutland Place 74

St Barnabas Church 81
St James Chapel for Seamen 46
St Joseph's Primary School 92
St Michael's Church 46, 78, 79
St Michael's Drum and Fife Band 107
St Michael's School 48, 54, 91
St Michael's Street 91, 103
St Paul's Church 57, 81, 112, 114
St Peter's Church 79-81
St Stephen's Church 64, 67, 68
St Stephen's Church Mission 54, 68
Salutation Inn 9, 10, 12, 38, 55
Schools 90-92
Seamen's Bethel, Williams Street 36, 40, 46, 47, 82
Seamen's Home 39, 42, 44, 51, 52
Setterland, George 85
Shaw, G B 110, 111
Shea, Jerry 117, 118
Ship Hotel 94
Ship Lane 103
Sickert, Walter 111
South Market Street 101
South Wales Argus 115
Speedwell Street 103
Springfield Well 94
Spring Gardens School 92
Spurgeon, Rev C H 40, 72, 85
Stares, Rev Brian 68
Stradling, Sir Henry 101
Street Life 96, 97
Street Names 101-103
Stringer, Rev J 77
Sunni and Shea Sects 84
Synagague 46, 47, 83

Taylor, Henry 90
Temple Street 11, 15, 22, 57, 70, 79, 90, 94, 101, 111, 123
Thatcher's Brewery 93

Thomas, Rev Ben 71
Thomas, Chris 72
Thomas, Rev Cyril 76
Thomas, Rev D J 72
Thomas, Rev Evan 70, 71, 108
Thomas, Rt Hon J H 51, 112-114
Thomas, Rev J Pardoe 72, 74
Thorn, James 66
Thorne, Alfred 98
Town Dock 10-14, 20-22, 24-26, 28-31, 34, 40, 42, 55, 56, 58, 94, 96, 104-106
Transporter Bridge 45, 86, 87, 89, 98-100
Travers, George 120
Travers, Wm 120
Tredegar Arms Hotel 11
Tredegar Dry Dock 56
Tredegar, Lady 106
Tredegar, Lord 32, 45, 53, 81, 87, 88, 92, 112, 123
"Tredegar of Newport" 104
Tredegar Wharf 9, 22
Tredegar Wharf Co 9, 56, 58, 65, 67, 85, 95
Tredegar Wharf School 49, 50, 91
Trinity School 27, 28, 34, 36, 90, 109
Trinity Girls School 29, 36, 109
Trinity Independent Chapel 18, 23, 90
Troop, Rev Fr 79
Turnpike Road 62
Tyack, Ald R S 112
Typhus 15, 50

Union Inn 9
United Methodist Church 66
Upper Lewis Street 51, 109
Upper Raglan Street 52
Ushiro Judo Club 92, 120, 121

Uskside Co 23, 41

Voluntary Schools 90, 91

Wallis Street 114
Watchhouse Parade 68, 101
Watchhouse, The 22
Waterloo Gate 95
Waterloo Road 87
Water Sellers 12, 94, 95
Water Supply 16, 17, 94
Watkins, "Gran" 95
Wedlake Court 103
Welsh Baptist Church 13, 14, 19, 23, 64, 65
Welsh Baseball Association 116
Welsh Calvinistic Chapel — see Ebenezer Church
Welsh National Eisteddfod 86, 88
Wesley, Rev John 61
Wesleyan Methodist Church 10, 19, 63, 64, 77
Wesleyan Methodist Day School 16, 39, 64, 90
Wesleyan Reformers 25, 69
West Market Street 101
Wharfs 55
Whitefield, Rev 61
Wilde, Jimmy 116
Williams, Rev W H 72
Williams Street 43, 52, 57, 91, 102
Wingate Street 102
Wolesley Street 52, 102
Workingen's Institute 29-31, 34
Wravall, Wm 104
Wright, Coun Peter 107, 108

Y Demel Chapel—see Welsh Baptist Chapel
YMCA, Temple Street 116
York Place (Pill) 103
Young's Shipbuilding Yard 10, 18

Sources of Information

Most of the research for this book has been done by meticulously and patiently "thumbing" through old newspapers found in the Newport Reference Library, such as the *Weekly* and *South Wales Argus,* the *Monmouthshire Merlin,* the *Star of Gwent* and the *Newport Gazette,* so that, as far as possible, the information could be original and accurate.

One other source of information which has been particularly helpful is *Parker's Bibliography of Newport* which is recommended to all students whose task it is to write anything on Newport. It is readily available in the Newport Reference Library, John Frost Square, as are most of the publications hereafter mentioned: —

Pill Area Survey published by the Council in 1964.

Pill Area Survey and Proposals published by the Council in 1969.

Rise and Progress of Newport by Ald H J Davis printed 1891.

Historic Newport by James Matthews.

Trams and Buses of Newport 1845-1981 by D B Thomas & E A Thomas.

Newport Transport 80 Years of Service by E A Thomas.

Catholic Churches and Schools by Cyril F Bates.

Wesleyan Methodist Churches—Official Handbook to the Rainbow Bazaar (1907. (Includes an account of Methodism in Newport from 1896-1907.)

History of Commercial Road Baptist Church by R J Langmaid.

Jubilee Celebrations—Alma Street Baptist Church 1916.

Centenary Celebrations—Alma Street Baptist Church 1966.

Annual Reports 1887-1931 Demyl Welsh Baptist Church, Commercial Road.

Catholicism in Newport by J H Canning.

Mission to Seamen Annual Reports 1945-66 and Quarterly Bulletins 1948-49.

Newport Hebrew Congregation.

Early Non-Conformity in Newport.

Churches in Newport 1930.

Sources of Information—continued

The Royal National Eisteddfod of Wales—Newport 1897. Official Programme. Geo Bell.

The Royal National Eisteddfod of Wales—Newport 1897. Letter Book 15 April 1877—12 August 1897.

History of Education 1904-1954.

The Super Tramp (W H Davies) by Sybil Hollingdrake MA. (Also many other references in Parker's Bibliography.)

When Labour Rules by J H Thomas MP.

My Story by J H Thomas MP.

Report to Secretary of State on Disaster at Alexandra Docks on 2 July 1909 by W W Squires.

Docks Extension Disaster 1909—Boy Hero Lewis.

"Pill-box" Magazine produced by the Polypill Group since July 1971.

"Community News" produced by the Pill Advice Centre from August 1974 to March 1982.

Who's Who in Newport—Wm Press Ltd 1920.

Acts for Making, Maintaining and Extending a Dock (Old Town Dock) 1840 and 1858—George Eyre and Spottiswoode.

Alexandra Dock and Railway Co. The largest dock in the world—souvenir programme of opening ceremony of new lock (includes history of Alexandra Docks).

Street Directories and Almanacks from 1857.

Judo Motion in Poetry by F E A Yates (Starling Press 1981).

Much information has also been obtained from interviewing older residents of Pillgwenlly and from many books and leaflets from *Parker's Bibliography* which are far too many to list here.

" Pillgwenlly " Newport—Vol. II

TO BE PUBLISHED IN 1984

1 Diary of Events 1876-1950.

2 The Royal Gwent Hospital from its days as an Infirmary in Llanarth Street in 1838.

3 The Police and the Fire Service from 1836 when all the local government services were administered by the Police (including fire-fighting).

4 Pillgwenlly during the two world wars.

5 The Politics of Pillgwenlly from the time when there was no Labour Party, and candidates would stand as "Roman Catholic" or "Wesleyan Methodist".

6 More Sport including Pigeon Racing.

7 Industry from the time when cannons were made at the Uskside Company, Church Street.

8 Pubs, Shops, Clubs and Cinemas including the notorious Beer Houses.

9 Carnivals & Festivals 1977-79. When Pillgwenlly residents let their hair down.

10 The Youth of Pillgwenlly.

11 Some more well-known characters including Joseph Latch, Newport's first Mayor and Father Hill.

STARLING PRESS LTD . RISCA . NEWPORT . GWENT . UK
(Tel 0633 612251)   **Publisher-in-Chief: F E A Yates**

ORDER DIRECT OR FROM YOUR BOOKSHOP : Stocks November 1983

STARLING PRESS PUBLICATIONS—MAIN STOCKISTS—GREAT BRITAIN are:—
W H SMITH & SON LTD countrywide
H J LEAR LTD 13-17 ROYAL ARCADE CARDIFF CF1 2PR
ORIEL, CHARLES STREET, CARDIFF
WELSH BOOKS COUNCIL — ABERYSTWYTH — WALES

UNITED STATES OF AMERICA ALSO CANADA:—
MARK SLATER, THE WELSH DRAGON, 211 MAIN ST.
ANNAPOLIS, MARYLAND 21401, USA
Tel: 301 267 8491

SOUTH WALES BOOKS MY SCENE by F E A Yates 1978 Reprint 1983
ISBN 0 903434 32 6 Text/Photos 107pp Paperback £1
This is a personal account by the Managing Director describing the contents of 19 books published by Starling Press, as well as anecdotes concerning events during the preparation for production. Interesting to possess if reader has any of the books.

SOUTH WALES BOOKS SCENE TWO due in January 1984. Deals with most of remaining titles on our lists. £1.50.

TREDEGAR MY TOWN by W C Smith & F E A Yates 1976 & 1982
ISBN 0 903434 25 3 Text/Photos 115pp Paperback £2.70 (Reprint 1982)
Jottings of W C Smith were edited by F E A Yates.

RAGLAN CASTLE by H Durant 1980
ISBN 0 903434 41 5 Text 100pp Photos 14pp Paperback £3

PENARTH A HISTORY by Roy Thorne 1975 & 1982
ISBN 0 903434 04 0 Text 84pp Photos 44pp Paperback £3.50

HISTORY OF PENARTH VOL 1 & 2 by Roy Thorne 1982
ISBN 0 903434 55 5 Text 204pp Photos 194pp Casebound £6.50
Stocks at SNELL in PENARTH.

A GOOD HEAD FOR BEER by Gareth D John 1982
ISBN 0 903434 52 0 Text 224pp 31 photos Casebound £6.50

This is a book for every beer enthusiast. It proves to be a fascinating historical background of beer as well as explaining the brewing process and ingredients used. There is a full coverage of all breweries in the UK and names Home Brew Pubs of delight to CAMRA enthusiasts. Written by a talented well qualified author Gareth D John BSc MSc PhD CChem MRSC onetime of Ynysddu and Pontllanfraith Grammar/Tech School.

THE CHARTIST MOVEMENT IN MONMOUTHSHIRE by James Davies 1982
ISBN 0 903434 45 8 Text 51pp Photos 24pp Casebound £3.60
Illustrations collected by F E A Yates for this edition of 1982.

MAD GERRY, WELSH WARTIME MEDICAL OFFICER by Gerald F Petty 1982
ISBN 0 903434 47 4 Text 142pp Photos 24pp Casebound £5
Dr Petty is a well known resident in Llandaff, Cardiff who until his retirement had a very large practice in the capital city. This is his true story of his RAMC service.

GLIMPSES OF OLD DINAS POWYS by Chrystal Tilney 1982
ISBN 0 903434 49 0 Text 164pp (230 photos) Casebound £6.50

DINAS POWYS RFC 1882-1982 by A Moses & B Moses 1982
ISBN 0 903434 56 3 Text 150pp Photos 70pp Casebound £6.50
Tony Moses, PhD and his wife Brenda Moses, BSc

THE PLACE NAMES OF GWENT by Canon E T Davies 1982 £1.50
ISBN 0 903434 50 4 Text 36pp Booklet

TRAMS AND BUSES OF NEWPORT (1845 to 1981) by D Thomas & E A Thomas 1982
ISBN 0 903434 48 2 Text 104pp Photos 112pp Casebound £6.90

GLAMORGAN—ITS GENTLEMEN & YEOMANRY 1797 to 1980 by Bryn Owen 1983
ISBN 0 903434 61 X Text 139pp Photos 54pp Casebound £6.50
BRYN OWEN is Honorary Curator of The Welch Regiment Museum at Cardiff Castle :
Lieutenant RN (Retd) : Expert in Welsh Military History.

CRUISING ALONG THE MON & BREC CANAL by James Eyles
Text 40pp Photos 16pp Paperback 60p 1972 and reprinted annually

---

BASSALEG SCHOOL DIARY TO 1979 by Joan Lougher 1983
ISBN 0 903434 60 1 Text 95pp Photos 46pp Paperback £4.50

PONTYPRIDD SOUTH: PAST & PRESENT by D J Rees 1983
ISBN 0 903434 54 7 Text 197pp Photos 32pp Casebound £6.50

RISCA RUGBY DAYS OF GLORY by Jack Strickland 1983
ISBN 0 903434 57 1 Text 85pp Photos 36pp Casebound £4.50

LOONY LIMERICKS OF BBC RADIO WALES 1983
ISBN 0 903434 65 2 160pp: 420 limericks Paperback £1.50
Chosen from 10,000 sent in by listeners of The Mike Flynn Radio Show

---

BASSALEG RECOLLECTIONS by F E A Yates 1983
ISBN 0 903434 59 8 Casebound £5.50
Includes Gwilym's Garden by **Gwilym Maesaleg**; excerpts from **Between Mountain and Marsh** by Antony Pickford; articles and photos from local residents.

MY LIFE THROUGH SIX REIGNS by W G Curtis Morgan 1983
ISBN 0 903434 70 9 Text 120pp Casebound £6.50

W G Curtis Morgan was born in 1892 at Talybont, near Aberystwyth, and since 1946 he has lived in Llandovery. Actual experiences in Queen's College Oxford, South Wales Borderers 1915, Indian Army 1918, travels in China, Japan, North America, Wimbledon tennis 1930, World War 2 in RAF; fascinating personal life.

RHYMNEY VALLEY ALBUM by Hilda M Evans 1983
ISBN 0 903434 58 X Casebound £5.50

Well known local resident. This 240pp Album has 405 numbered photos and text. Ten villages featured from Aberbargoed to Troedrhiwfuch.
Author of NEW TREDEGAR IN FOCUS (1977) and NEW TREDEGAR AGAIN (1979).

CAERLEON ENDOWED SCHOOL 1724-1983 by T M Morgan 1983
ISBN 0 903434 75 X Text 100pp Casebound £4

Trevor Morris Morgan was Director of Education, Monmouthshire & Gwent from 1956 to 1976. Events of major significance in the history of Education are reflected in this narrative. Caerleon is on the outskirts of Newport, Gwent.

PILLGWENLLY: NEWPORT by Cliff Knight 1983
ISBN 0 903434 85 7 Text 132pp and 258 Photos Casebound £6.50

SISTER PEGGIE'S NOTEBOOK by Ethel Dearden 1983
ISBN 0 903434 80 6 Text 141pp and 16pp Photos Paperback £4.50

STARLING PRESS LTD . RISCA . NEWPORT . GWENT . UK
(Tel 0633 612251)   **Publisher-in-Chief: F E A Yates**

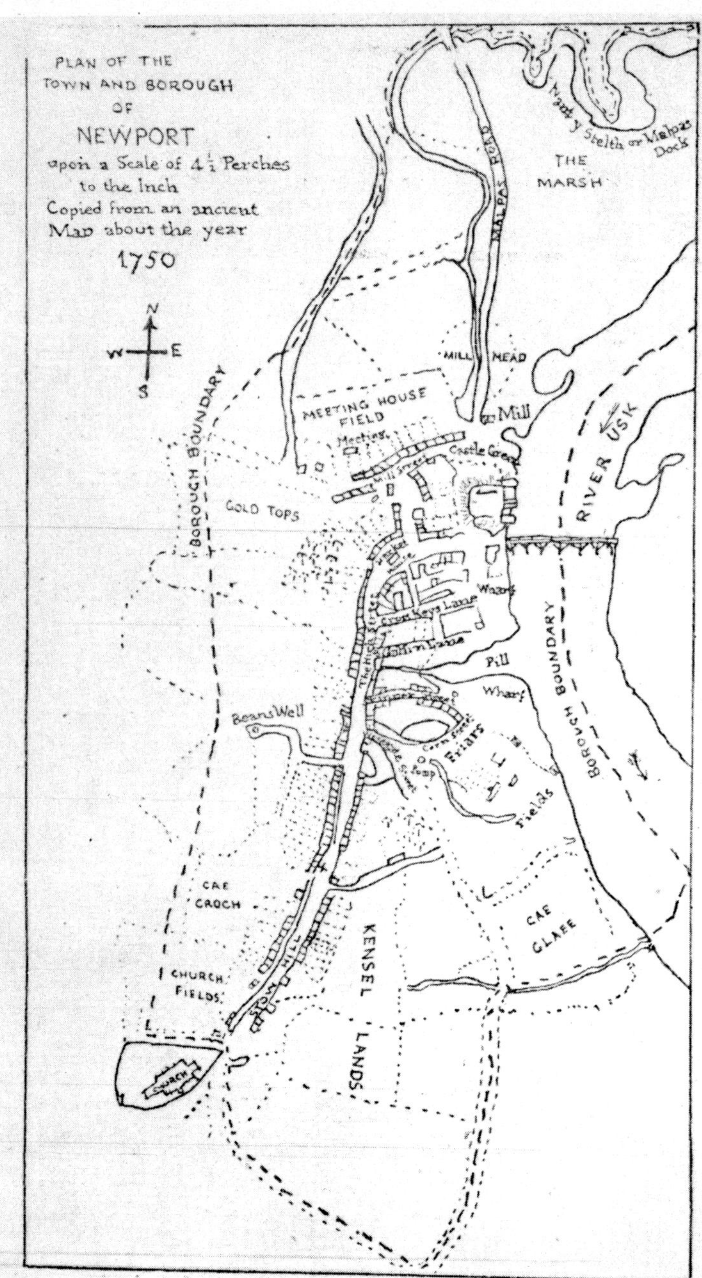

1—Plan of Newport 1750.

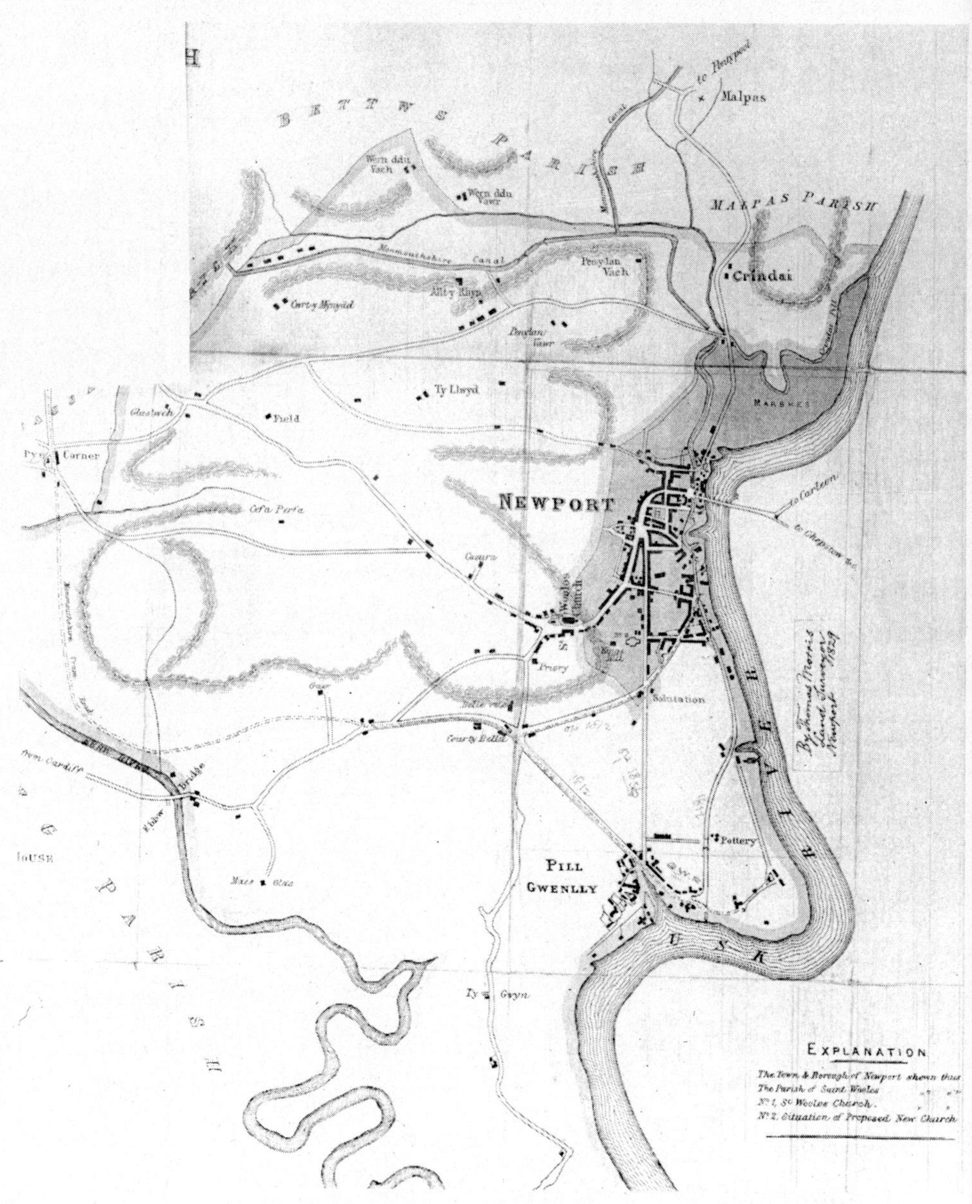

2—Plan of Newport 1829.

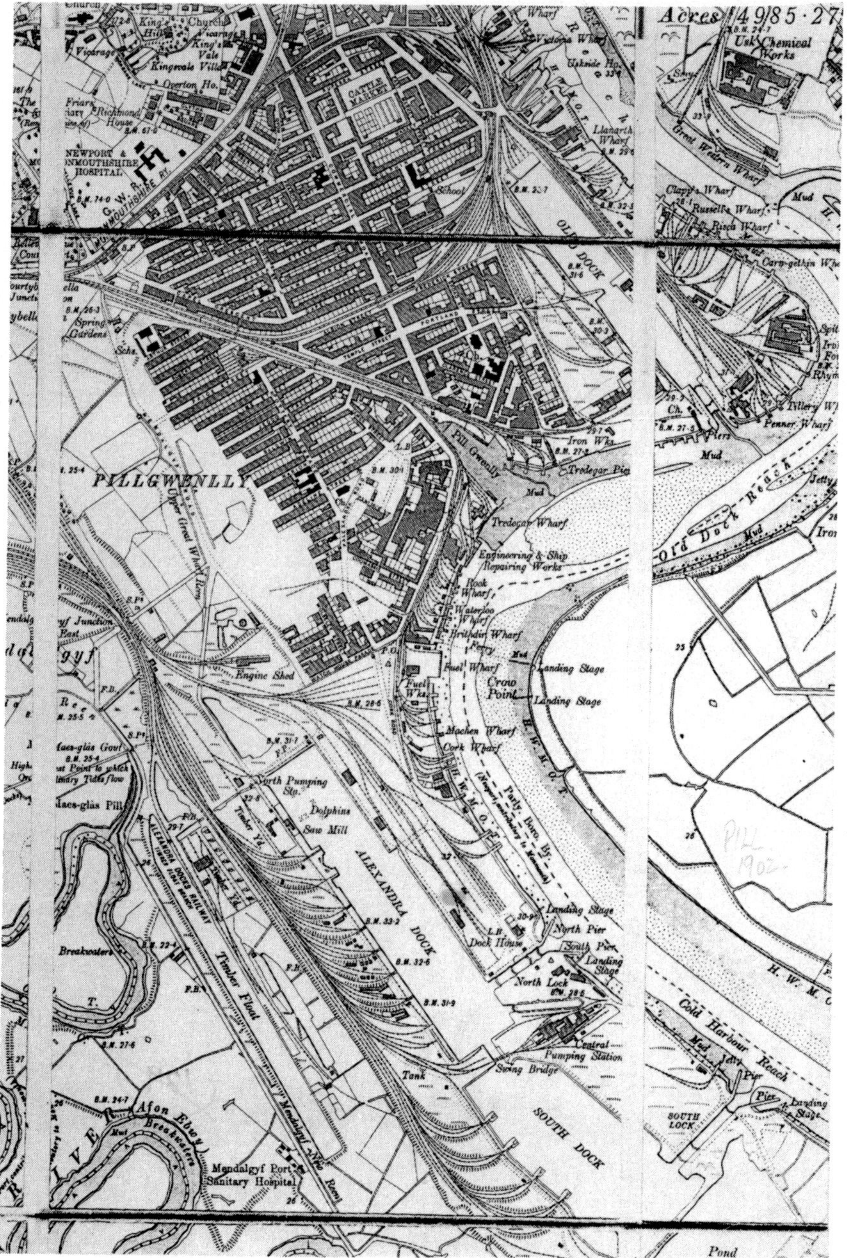

3—Plan of Pillgwenlly 1902 showing the Old Town Dock and railways running along Cardiff Road and George Street.

4—General view of Newport 1875; the year of the opening of the Alexandra Dock.

5—General view of Pillgwenlly about 1908.

6—Aerial view of Pillgwenlly about 1920 showing the Old Town Dock, the Cattle Market
and the River Wharves.

7—Coal hoists Alexandra Dock. About 1920.

8—Aerial view of South Pill about 1920 showing Pill Harriers Grounds, Batchelors Timber Yard, and the Mendalgief Road Recreation Ground.

9—Horse drawn tram at Pill Gates about 1900. Ship Hotel (now Alexandra Court Flats) in the background.

10—Ale being transported by steam.

11—The way coal was delivered in the early 1900's.

12—Carriage built in Pillgwenlly in the late 1800's.

13—James Parry delivering coal in 1935.

14—Delivery van belonging to Griffiths & Sons of George Street and Commercial Road. About 1910.

15—Off for a trip to the sea from the Royal Oak PH Courtybella Terrace.
About 1900.

16—Funeral carriage outside A E Hicks premises in Charlotte Street.
About 1932.

17—Tram No 51 being brought back to Cashmores Yard for breaking up in 1937.

18—Annual Outing of Griffiths & Sons, George Street and Commercial Road in June 1907.

19—Hearse belonging to A E Hicks Ltd being driven into the Cattle Market prior to sale in 1932.

20—Funeral carriage belonging to A E Hicks arriving at the Cattle Market ready for sale in 1932.

21—One of the three Andrews Patent 'Buses supplied in 1886 to Edmund Perry. Late 1800's.

22.—Sir Joseph Lawrence Conservative MP for Newport in 1901 uses his vehicle for canvassing.

23—Wheelbarrows built in 1871 to carry coal from Courtybella Terrace when it was nine old pence per cwt.

24—Open top horse drawn trams crossing at the Iron Gates Railway Crossing Commercial Road/Frederick Street, about 1900.

25—2-8-0T steam locomotive No 4203 takes a goods train across the Iron Gates level crossing in August 1948. The Railways had been nationalised the previous January but the loco still carries the initials of the Great Western Railway.

26—Ebenezer Welsh Calvinistic (Presbyterian) Church), Commercial Road.

27—Commercial Road Wesleyan Chapel as it is today.

28—Commercial Road Wesleyan Sisterhood.

29—Sisterhood Trip from Commercial Road Wesleyan Chapel.

30—Welsh Baptist Temple, Commercial Road.

CHURCH OFFICERS.

Pastorate Vacant.

Deacons.

Mr. JOHN WILLIAMS, 25, Capel Street.

„ H. GIBBON, Temple Cottage.

„ ED. ROBERTS, 68 Lewis Street.

„ JOHN JOHN, 3 Beeches Cottages, Prince Street.

„ LEVI PHILLIPS, 33 Coldra Road.

Treasurer—

Mr. JNO. JOHN, 3 Beeches Cottages, Prince Street.

Secretary—

Mr. J. B. WILLIAMS, 29A Commercial Street

Conductors of Singing—

CONGREGATIONAL:	SUNDAY SCHOOL:
Mr. L. R. JONES,	Mr. WM. NATHAN,
6 Batchelor Road.	Temple Cottage.

Organist—

Mrs. M. L. WILLIAMS, 29A Commercial Street.

House Agent—

Mr. JNO. WILLIAMS, 25 Capel Street.

Pew Rent Collector—

Mr. T. BUCKLEY, Lucas Street.

Chapel Keeper—

Mr. R. PRITCHARD, Temple Cottage.

ORDER OF SERVICES.

Lord's Day at 10 a.m.	...	...	...	...	Prayer Meeting.
„ „ 11 „	...	...	...	...	Sermon.
„ „ 2.30 p.m. ...	...	...	..		School.
„ „ 6 „	...	...	...	...	Sermon.
*Monday Evening at 7.30	...	...	...	...	Society Meeting.
Thursday „ „	...	...	...	...	Prayer Meeting.

*On the first Monday in each month a Missionary Prayer Meeting will be held instead of the Society Meeting.

The Ordinance of the Lord's Supper will be celebrated at the close of the Evening Service each lunar month, commencing from January 24th, 1904.

31—Church Officers Welsh Baptist Temple 1904.

32—New Testament Church of God.

33—Plan showing the nearness of the Pillgwenlly Churches.

34—Holy Trinity Church Choir 1913. Includes Capt Parfitt (Church Warden); E G R Richards (Church Organist); Mr Langmaid; Ivor Wall; Arthur Jones; Reg Jones; Ivor Woods; Billy Powell; Arthur Woods.

35—St Stephen's Church Choir 1914/18 war.

36—Wedding of Mr John Clarke of 8 Temple Street at Holy Trinity Church September 1940.

37—Opening of New Hall at St Stephen's Church June 1974. Group includes:— The Mayor and Mayoress (Councillor and Mrs John Marsh); the Lord Bishop of Monmouth (Rev D G Childs); Rev John Douglas (Vicar); Rev David Hardiman (Minister of Alexandra Road Baptist Church); and Father Joseph Hassett (Priest at St Michael's Roman Catholic Church).

38—Holy Trinity Church during demolition September 1977.

39—Induction of the Rev Brian Stares as Vicar of St Stephens 1977. Left to right: Canon W C Ponton; Very Rev Frank Jenkins (Dean of St Woolos); Capt Derek Jones (Church Army); Mr R C Greenland (Church Warden); the Lord Bishop of Monmouth—Rev D G Childs; Mr R S G Williams (Diocesan Registrar); Rev Brian M W Stares; Mr J H Egan (Church Warden); Mr W Westwood (Parish Lay Reader); Ven Cecil Willis (Archdeacon of Newport).

40—St Stephens Church showing main entrance from Adeline Street.

41—"Live" TV Service at St Stephens Church 25th November 1979.

42—Parry Family Trip to Bath and Wells (Most of the Parry Family were members of the Portland Street United Methodist Free Church). 1. James Parry (Coal Merchant, 30 Mill Parade); 2. His daughter Florence; 3. His wife Ada; 4. His brother George; 5. Tom Parry; 6. Emily Parry; 7. Mable Parry; 8. William Sully; 9 Sam Dart; 10. Emily Maud Parry; 11. Ted Tilley; 12. Ann Sully (wife of William); 13. Bertram Parry.

43—Portland Street Boys' Brigade AFC league champions 1909-10 (8th Newport Company).

44—Portland Street Sunday School on Whit Monday March 1920.

45—Portland Street Sunday School Anniversary Demonstration.
"The Transporter Bridge" early 1900's.

46—Portland Street Temperance Society protest against strong drink (note Phillips & Sons Brewery in background) early 1900's.

47—James Parry of Mill Parade. Leading member of Portland Street Church.

48—The Carpenters Shop in Portland Street where Commercial Road Baptist Church started in 1860.

49—The Dolphin Street Mission started by Commercial Road Baptist Church in 1893. Rebuilt 1907.

50—The Commercial Road Baptist Church (Now—1983 a Superstore).

51—Commercial Road Baptist Sunday School. Winners of the Scripture Examination Shield. About 1960. Photograph includes Doug Webb; George Thomas; Olwyn Webb; Vi Watkins; Jean Thomas; Olive Harding; Joycelyn Watkins; Bryn Hayman; Roy Colman; Nancy Griffiths; Roslyn Webb; Lynne Elliott; Robert Chicken; Gaynor Shepstone; Derek Netherway; Donald Elliott; Olive Thomas; Mr Smith; Mr Hayman and others.

52—Commerical Road Baptist Church Choir 1937.

53—Pastors and Officers, Alma Street Baptist Church. Early 1900's.

54—Interior Alma Street Baptist Church. About 1890.

55—Senior members Alma Street Baptist Sunday School 1918.

Back Row: Fred Jones; Mr Dunn; A Coes; Mr Skinner; A Thomas; N Pugh. **Second Row:** Mrs Lovelock; Miss A Jeffries; Mrs Davies; Mrs Langford; Miss A Jones; Miss J Marsh; Miss H Thomas; Mrs A Coes; Miss M Thomas; Mrs Grainger; Miss G Jones; Mr William Jones; Miss L Jones. **Third Row:** Mrs Bath; Mr W R Thomas; Mr Chris Thomas; Mrs G Harris; Rev Griffith Harris; Mrs W Morgan; Mr W Morgan; Mrs Marsh. **Front Row:** Miss D Comeford; Miss G Hughes; Miss N Jones; Miss E Beddis; Miss E Jones; Miss A Jones; Miss W Bath; Miss D Green.

56—Miss May Thomas's Sunday School Class. Alma Street Baptist Church. About 1930.

Back Row: T Capel; J Jones; L Gabb; J Marshall. Second Row: E Rowlands; E Jeffries-Marshall; R Morris; J Bishop; J Samson; J Pugsley; R Panting. **Front Row:** B Pearce; E Lawrence; Miss May Thomas (Leader); C Harris; P Hughes.

57—Alma Street Baptist Sunday School Whitsuntide March 1944. (Alma Street —junction with Charlotte Street.)

58—Alma Street Baptist Sunday School. Scripture Examination Shield Winners.
About 1945.

Back Row: Rev & Mrs B J Allsopp and Miss N Luxton (Leaders). **Second Row:** Stanley Seaman; Maurice Oliver; Margery Knight; May Clark; Margaret Webb; Avril Palmer; Joan Hughes; Margery Lewis; Muriel Seaman; Olga Seaman. **Third Row:** Kenneth Hughes; Gerald Palmer. **Fourth Row:** Pat Sweet; Margaret Williams; Marlene Upton; Greta Satchell; Mary Springthorpe; Helena Keene; Anne Springthorpe; Gloria Glover; Ann Thomas; Margaret Seaman; June Thomas; Valerie Johnson; Beryl Johnson. Front Row: Peter Saunders; Eric Palmer.

59—Mr Walter Thomas's Sunday School Class. (Alma Street Church.)
About 1960.

Back Row: Ken Dumayne; Richard Jones; Roger Richardson; Nick Hutchings. **Second Row:** Ken Sheppard; Derek Shinton; Bryan Tomkins; Alan Jones. **Front Row:** David Kingston; Jeremy Knight; Norman Price.

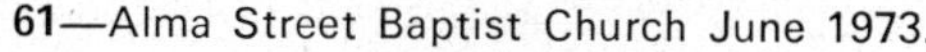

60—Interior Alma Street Baptist Church just before demolition in May 1976.

61—Alma Street Baptist Church June 1973.

62—Pastor and Deacons, Alma Street Baptist Church. About 1975.

Back Row: Richard Jones; Digby Williams; Roy Jenkins; Chas Jones; Allan Parry; David Waring; Stan Capel. Front Row: Cliff Knight; Jeff Nowell; Rev Graham Harrison, MA, B Litt (Pastor); Phil Watson.

63—Alma Street Baptist Chapel being demolished May 1976.

64—Setting out the new Alma Street Church (to be called Emmanuel Evangelical Church) before building commenced in October 1976. (Royal Gwent Hospital in background.)

65—The new Chapel being built June 1977.

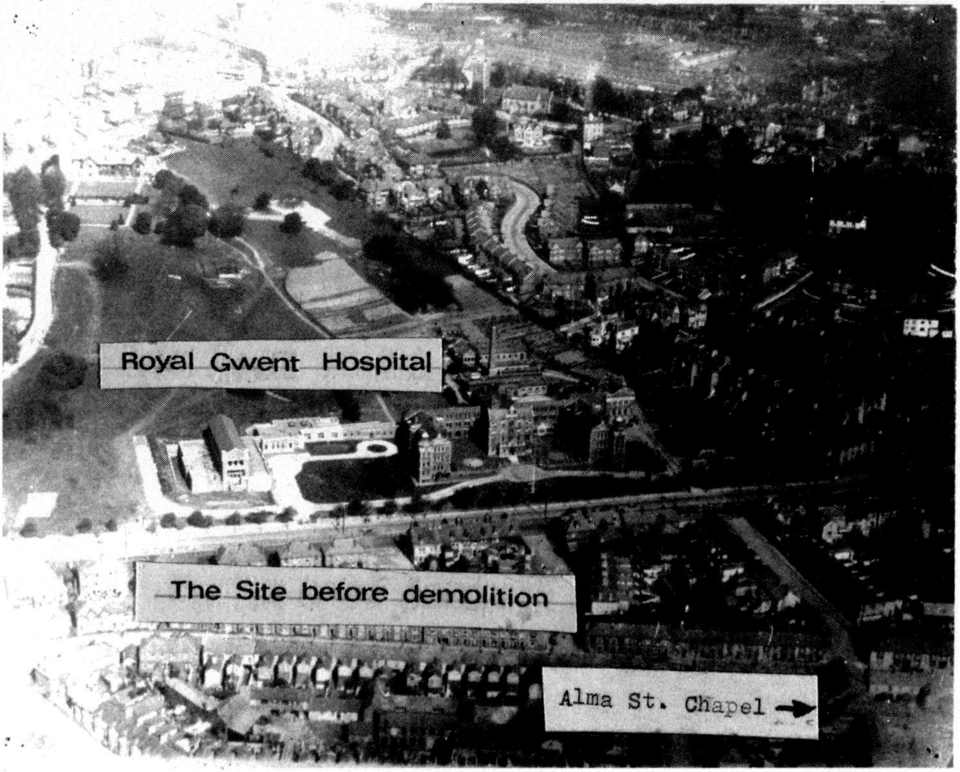

66—Aerial View showing site of Emmanuel Chapel. (Royal Gwent Hospital and Dewsland Park Road in background.) Photo taken about 1920.

67—Emmanuel Evangelical Church as seen from Rutland Place.

68—Interior Emmanuel Chapel.

69—A group of young people outside the Chapel (note number of "immigrant" children).

70—The Old Mountjoy Street Gospel Hall.

Order of

BROADCAST
SERVICE

from

MOUNTJOY STREET HALL

MOUNTJOY STREET
NEWPORT, MON.

SUNDAY
October 19th, 1958, at 7.45 p.m.

———

Welsh Home Service   B.B.C. Wavelength 341m.

Speaker: A. G. ANSTICE

Organist: B. Mervyn George   Hymn Leader: W. P. Parry

Hymns from Sankey's 1200 Hymn Book

72—Group inside the Church 1960.

73—The new Mountjoy Gospel Hall in course of construction March 1982.

74—The Gospel Hall completed.

75—Alexandra Road Baptist Church.

76—Alexandra Road Guild Cricket Club 1912.

Back Row: E Roberts; R H Goulding; C Ham; W Yeo. **Second Row:** T Gibson; J Wood; T Roberts; G Williams. **Third Row:** G C Miller; F Card; J A Essery (Capt); R George; A J Morgan. **Sitting:** J M Reynolds (Scorer).

77—Alexandra Road Baptist Renovation Team 1926.
Back Row: Charlie Pithers; Tom Jones; Walter Sears; Bill Johnson. **Front Row:** George French; Arthur Williams; Joe Nowell; Vic Kerrell; Frank Walters.

78—Alexandra Road Baptist AFC 1928/29.

Back Row: Fred Hayward; Vic Kerrell; Reg Gray; Frank Walton; Eddie Bartlett; George Kerrell; Albert Vittle. **Middle Row:** George Thomas: George Bright; Rev D W Ingram; Eddie Vaughan; Arthur Evans. **Front Row:** Arthur Lawrence; Antice Rowe.

79—Alexandra Road Baptist Cricket Team 1930's.

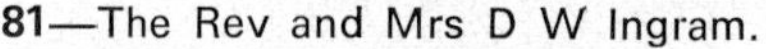

80—Building of new School Hall at Alexandra Road Baptist Church 1930's.
"Builders" include Rev D W Ingram (Pastor) and John Clark (Deacon).

81—The Rev and Mrs D W Ingram.

82—Price Street Methodist Church, Pottery Terrace, taken on the day of the Final Service 11 August 1978.

83—A group of Price Street Sisterhood taken in 1936. Includes: Mrs Ingleson; Mrs Elworthy; Mrs Gardner; Mrs Williams; Mrs Green and Mrs Brunskill.

84—Some of the congregation at the last service held at Price Street Methodist Church.

85—Price Street Methodist Church being demolished September 1978.

86—St Michael's RC Church, Clarence Street.

87—St Michael's Church Altar Boys. About 1930.

88—St Peter's Seamen's Church, Temple Street.

89—Interior of St Peter's Church.

90—Group of Sunday School Scholars taken outside St Peter's Church 1920's.

91—Another group taken outside the Church 1920's.

92—Mrs Molineux (Pastor's wife) with some of the girls from St Peter's Sunday School.

Group includes: Muriel Harvey; Marie Sweeting; Dorothy Rich; Peggy Mabe; Vera Bettws; Sheilah Healey; Phylis Betts Marjory Ingleson; Ivy Rowland; Joyce Henners; Edna Sweeting; Florence Newsay; Lesley Betts.

93—St Peter's Church being demolished. March 1981) taken from Albion Street).

94—St Barnabas Church, New Ruperra Street.

95—Opening ceremony at the Seamen's Mission, Alexandra Dock 1951.

96—Choir at the opening of the Seamen's Mission, Alexandra Dock 1951.

97—The Jewish Synagogue, Lewis Street/Francis Street.

98—The Synagogue being demolished September 1973.

99—Opening of the new Mosque in Commercial Road July 1982 by Councillor John Pembridge, Chairman of Newport Planning Committee.

100—The Pakistan Ambassador visits the Mosque. Also in the photograph—Mr Roy Hughes MP and the Mayor of Newport (Councillor Mrs Ruby Kehmstedt).

100A—(During the 1920's) Children of Frederick Street pose for the camera. Note how poorly clad: some without shoes and socks.

CYMDEITHAS YR IAITH GYMRAEG

Mewn Cysylltiad a Chymdeithas Anrhydeddus y Cymmrodorion.

* CYNHELIR *

CYFARFOD ⊹ BLYNYDDOL

Y GYMDEITHAS UCHOD YN YR

YSGOL SIR I FERCHED.

CASNEWYDD,

Dydd Mercher, Awst 4, 1897, am Bump o'r gloch

. . . DARLLENIR PAPYR AR . . .

"LLE Y CYMRAEG MEWN ADDYSG,"

. . . GAN . . .

W. Lewis Jones, Ysw., M.A., Bangor

Gellir cael pob hysbysrwydd pellach oddiwrth yr Ysgrifenydd,

L. D. JONES,

3, Edge Hill,

Garth, Bang'

101—Notice of opening of Welsh National Eisteddfod at the Cattle Market 1897.

THE
ROYAL NATIONAL EISTEDDFOD
ᔆ 1897, ᔆ
THE PAVILION, NEWPORT.

Admission.

Reserved Seats.	Season Ticket, 9 Meetings, Transferable	30/-
Do	Single Meeting or Concert	5/-
1st Class.	Season Ticket, 9 Meetings, (Not Transferable)	21/-
Do.	Single Meeting or Concert	3/-
2nd Class.	Season Ticket, 9 Meetings, (Not Transferable)	12/6
Do.	Single Meeting or Concert	2/-
3rd Class.	Single Meeting or Concert	1/-

Admission to Military Band Contest, in Tredegar Hall, at 2 p m, Monday afternoon, Aug. 2nd **6d**

For full particulars of above apply to Messrs. Newman & Sons, Music Publishers Newport, where Reserved and Season Tickets may be obtained and Plan of Seats seen

Cheque or Postal Order must accompany each application for tickets ; otherwise owing to the great demand anticipated, the Committee cannot in any case reserve Seats or send Tickets.

Reserved and Season Tickets can only be obtained up to 10 a.m. on Monday August 2nd, after which they can only be obtained at the Reserved Entrance Booth

The 1st and 2nd Single Tickets can be obtained **only** at the Ticket Booths a the Entrance, during the Eisteddfod.

The Booths will be open **one hour** before each meeting.

No change given at the Ticket Booths, but may be obtained at a Specia Booth near at hand, provided for that purpose.

Carriage Entrance—Ruperra Street only.

Passes out from Pavilion Building into the Grounds—**Free.**

Passes out into the town—**Free.** Re-entry to the Grounds by Specia Pass Tickets, 3d each, which must be **obtained inside the Grounds befor leaving**.

No " Passes out " or re-admission allowed after **2** o'clock each day.

Refreshments will be provided within the Eisteddfod Grounds.

Special Trains returning after Evening Concerts will be run by the Railwa Companies. For Particulars see Railway Bills.

The Eisteddfod Day Meetings commence at **10.**

The Evening Concerts commence at **7.30.**

102—Prices of admission, etc, to the Eisteddfod.

103—Plan of the Eisteddfod.

Daniel Street.

No. of Street.		ACCOMMODATION. No. of Persons.	TARIFF. Bed & Br'kfast per day for 1 P.* s. d.		2 P.† s. d.	
5	Miss Evans	2	4	0		
11	Mrs. Hutchins	2	4	0		

Francis Street.

No. of Street.		No. of Persons.	1 P. s.	d.	2 P. s.	d.
6	Mrs. Bowen	6	4	0	7	6

Lewis Street.

No. of Street.		No. of Persons.	1 P. s.	d.	2 P. s.	d.
14	Mrs. Edmunds	2	4	0	7	6
24	„ Barton	2	4	0	7	6
41	„ Bolt	2	4	0	7	6
72	„ Dartnell	5	4	0	7	6
59	„ Fallows	2	3	6		
4	„ Smith	6	5	0	9	0
96	„ Redman	2	4	0	7	6
21	„ Beddis	2	4	0	7	6
32	„ Collins	2	4	0	7	6
31	„ Roderick	4	4	0	7	6
35	„ Rowe	2	4	0	7	6
92	„ Townsend	4	4	0	7	6
29	„ Pratten	2	4	0	7	6
62	„ Cook	2	4	0	7	6
104	„ Evans	2				
80	„ Macey	2	3	6		
11	„ Jones	4	4	0	7	6
9	„ Smith	3	4	0	7	6
25	„ Williams	3	4	0	7	6

William Street.

No. of Street.		No. of Persons.	1 P. s.	d.	2 P. s.	d.
3	Mrs. Thomas	4	4	0	7	6
35	„ Attewell	4	5	0	9	0
77	„ Panting	3	4	0	7	6
79	„ Oakley	4	4	0	7	6
5	„ Murrow	4	4	0	7	6
66	„ Madsen	4	4	0	7	6
41	„ Morgan	4	4	0	7	6
82	„ Pearce	2	6	0		
7	„ Fortune	6	4	0	7	6

Price Street.

No. of Street.		No. of Persons.	1 P. s.	d.	2 P. s.	d.
33	Mrs. Reed	4	3	6		
58	„ Samson	2	3	6		
61	„ Thomas	4	4	0		
74	„ Perkins	4	4	0		

Alice Street, Pillgwenlly.

No. of Street.		No. of Persons.	1 P. s.	d.	2 P. s.	d.
20	Mrs. Punchard	6	4	6	8	0
11	„ George	4	4	6	8	0
7	„ Teschner	4	4	6	8	0
13	„ Beer	4	4	6	8	0
22	„ Hook	2	4	6	8	0
16	„ Thomas	2	4	6	8	0
12	„ Jeens	4	4	6	8	0
1	„ Roberts	4	5	0		

* 1 person.   † 2 persons.

104—List showing accommodation available for visitors attending the Eisteddfod.

105 & 106—The Cattle Market today.

107—Cutting the first sod at Belle Vue Park by the Mayor Ald Henry John Davies 3 November 1892.

1. Harry John Davies (mayor).
2. Viscount Tredegar.
3. W. J. Lloyd.
4. Colonel C. Lyne.
5. Alderman Sam Batchelor
6. Mark Mordey
7.
8.
9. J. H. Carney
10. W. H. Brown
11. J. C. Saunders.
12. Archdeacon Bruce
13.
14.
15. Liscombe
16.
17. J. Firbank
18. R. Berry (Western Mail)
19. Alderman J. W. Jones (London Jones)
20. Dr George Davies
21. Hopkins (Western Mail)
22.
23. Jacobs
24.
25. Charles Wiles
26.
27.
28. James Saunders
29. Ed. Williams (Echo Williams)
30. Sinclair (Chief Constable).
31. Trace
32. Robert Wilkinson
33. Alderman H. J. Parnall
34. A. J. Spear (Town Clerk's Dept).
35. A. A. Newman (Town Clerk)
36. Alderman Enoch Griffiths
37. Alderman John Moses
38.
39. T. H. Howells
40.
41. Alderman Greenland
42. A. R. Bear
43.
44. Gill Williams
45. Alderman Tom Jones
46. Conyers Kirby (Boro Engineer)
47. J. Collins (Town Hall Keeper).
48. Arthur Batchelor
49. John Say (Corp. Road Inspector)
50. C. D. Phillips.
51. Cordey.
52.

108—Names of those attending the cutting of the first sod at Belle Vue Park.

The Transporter Bridge from Belle Vue Park, Newport, Mon.

109—A view from the bandstand Belle Vue Park about 1910 showing Spring Gardens Allotments where Whiteheads Works were later built.

110—Belle Vue Park just after it was opened in 1894.

111—The Gorsedd Stones at Belle Vue Park.

112—The Gorsedd Ceremony at Belle Vue Park 1897.

113—Trinity Voluntary School as it is today.

114—Class at St Michael's School. About 1920.

115—Some of the pupils of St Michael's School in the 1960's.
Back Row: B M Grime T Charlton; G Parelli; A Parfitt; P Flynn; M Hicks; S Gellyrice; R Saysell; F Zara; P Murray; A Leo. **Second Row:** S Castle; S McCarthy; K Thompson; C Griffin; R Vinigurra; P Givvons; M Centracchio; J Marshall; S Horsfield; M Ingego; M Flynn. **Third Row:** J Marney; C O'Flaherty; A Poretta; M Benettoni; R Prosperi; A Pisani; C O'Connor; A Cody. **Front Row:** M Murphy; C Gargaro; P Lavender; P Draper; J Wright; J Brunnock; H Shappard; S Holland.

116—Tredegar Wharf School taken at the time of the demolition of the Williams Street houses.

117—Tredegar Wharf School scholars about 1930.
Group includes: Harry Ritter; Horace Hill; Charlie Powell; John Ormonde; Les Coulson; Stan Hayward; Jack Harvey; Dai Roberts; George Isberg; Ron Ford; Billy Higgins; George Verrinder; Stan Elliott.

118—Alexandra School Boys' Class. Late 1800's.

119—"The Japanese Girls" Alexandra School. About 1900.

120—Art Class Alexandra School taught by Miss Agnes Jordan. About 1918.
Back Row: N Cook, V Cankett, C Hulbert, M Waldren, J Carney, O Clarke, V Davies, P Hockey. **Second Row:** M Brooks, D Bright, O Watts. **Third Row:** G Durrant, E Noakes, Miss Jorden, L Jones, R Edmunds. **Front Row:** V Basburn, O Thomas, V Davies.

121—Alexandra Infants 1922.

122—Alexandra Infants 1920's.

123—Alexandra Boys' Standard 1, 1920's. Teachers—Miss Boon and Mr Webb.

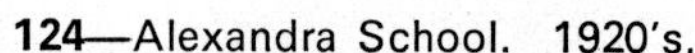

124—Alexandra School.   1920's.

125—Alexandra School. About 1931.

126—Alexandra School. About 1931.

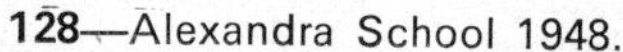

127—Alexandra School Standard 3 with their teacher Miss Theresa Barry 1940.

128—Alexandra School 1948.

129—Alexandra Road Soccer Team 1961/62.
Back Row: A N Other, C Shinton, A Bader, J Friend, D Johnsey, R Dowsell.   **Front Row:** L Cowen, L Nicholls, D Hopkins, A Mort, R Bright, B Periam.

130—Alexandra Road Primary School RFC. Seven-a-Side Winners 1974.
Back Row: Mr Mike Landers (Coach); Hassan Ali, Garry Urrutia, Philip Nichols, Jeffrey Pritchard, Alan Perret.   **Front Row:** Gordon Pitman, Paul Lewis, Andrew Perry (Capt), Robert Holland, Richard Tolley.

131—Bolt Street School today.

131A—Children of Alexandra School in Temple Street Library (during 1980) with their teacher Mr. Benson.

133—Stone carving on Bolt Street School Wall.

134—Belle Vue School (later Alexandra School) taken in 1982 at the time of the erection of the new houses in Arthur/Price Street.

135—Spring Gardens School (Standard II). About 1918.

136—Spring Gardens School. 14 year old leavers 1923.

137—Spring Gardens School Standard V about 1923.
(Some names missing throughout.) **Back Row:** McAngus, Joe Chapman, Channing, Orchard, Waggett, George Kenny. **Second Row:** Bunner Travers, Frank Rice, H Davies. **Third Row:** Roseblade; Holloway, Bob Grainger, Frank Glover, Fred Dullen, Morgan, W Beardmore. **Fourth Row:** Morgan, Andrew Grey, "Speggy" Bell, "Buller" Periam, F Snatchell, Les Hooper. **Front Row:** Ronnie Davies; Billy Morgan, Harry Gardner.

138—Believed to be Holy Cross School in the early 1900's.

139—Holy Cross Swimming Team with Father Honan. Winners of the Newport Schools Shield Competition 1928.

140—Holy Cross School Invincible Rugby Team 1935/36.
Back Row: Mr Tom Lenane, Danny Kerr, Frank Alonzi, Mike Alonzi, David Dowd, Bernard Croston, Gregory Williams, Father Honan. **Second Row:** David Jones, Tommy Chapman, Ivor Davis, Tommy Whitfield, George Thomas, Johnny Holland, Mike Sullivan. **Front Row:** John O'Neil; Johnny Kerr, Ken Goodwin, Johnny D'Arcy.

141—St Joseph's Primary School, Oswald Road, January 1976. Formerly Father Hills Memorial School.

141A—Ushiro Judo Club Leader, Bob Edwards (2nd Dan) seen with (on his left) his oldest pupil F E A Yates of The Starling Press Ltd (Orange Belt). The club functions in the Father Hills Memorial School, Oswald Road

142—Entrance to Thatchers Brewery, Alma Street, on extreme right (junction Herbert Street & Alma Street).

143—Drawing water from the well in Pillgwenlly mid 1800's.
(Artist's impression.)

144—How the Pillgwenlly ladies did their washing at the Canal in the mid 1800's. (Artist's impression.)

145—Water sellers in Pillgwenlly. Mid 1800's. (Artist's impression.)

146—Bon Fire Night in Pillgwenlly. About 1880. (Artist's impression.)

147—Horse-drawn Fire Engine in Pill late 1800's. (Artist's impression.)

74, ALMA STREET,

Newport, Mon., *July 4th* 192*8*

Miss Parry

Dr. to Miss B. England,

DRESSMAKER AND COSTUMIER.

Making Dress	8	6
Cotton & bow	1	3
	9	9

Settled with thanks
B. M. England

148—The cost of a hand made dress in 1928.

MACHEN WHARF,
or 39 Mill Parade,
NEWPORT,
190

Mr.

DEAR SIR,

We beg to call your attention to the following Price List for House Coals.

You will find **the prices compare favourably with any that can be offered elsewhere.** We assure you **the quality is equally favourable.**

We should be glad to give special quotations for large quantities

We can deliver the Coal in bags if required.

We remain,

Yours faithfully,

James Parry & Sons.

149—Coal, loose or in bags. Early 1900's.

150—The cost of being buried in 1882.

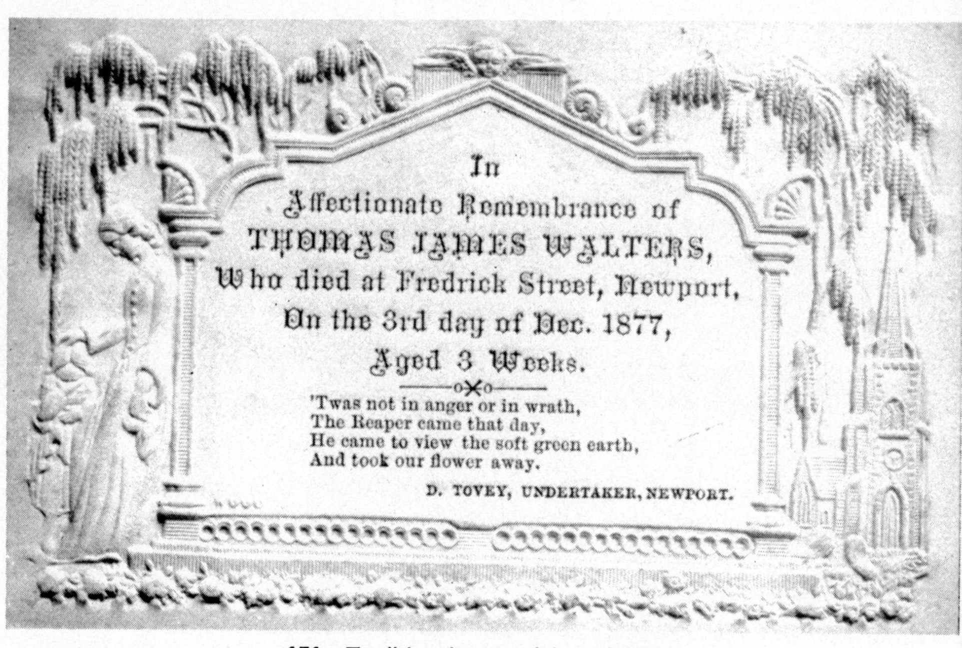

151—Traditional memorial card 1877.

152—When we paid the doctor 1893.

153—The Transporter Bridge from Alexandra Docks 1981.

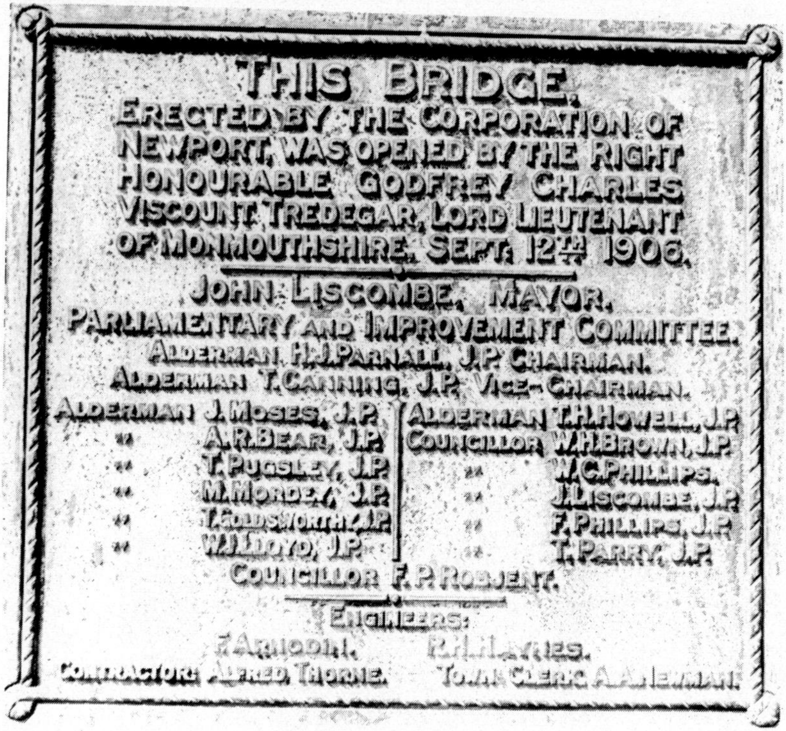

THIS BRIDGE,
ERECTED BY THE CORPORATION OF
NEWPORT, WAS OPENED BY THE RIGHT
HONOURABLE GODFREY CHARLES
VISCOUNT TREDEGAR, LORD LIEUTENANT
OF MONMOUTHSHIRE. SEPT. 12TH 1906.

JOHN LISCOMBE, MAYOR.
PARLIAMENTARY AND IMPROVEMENT COMMITTEE.
ALDERMAN H.J.PARNALL, J.P. CHAIRMAN.
ALDERMAN T.CANNING, J.P. VICE-CHAIRMAN.

ALDERMAN J.MOSES, J.P.   ALDERMAN T.H.HOWELL, J.P.
"   A.R.BEAR, J.P.   COUNCILLOR W.H.BROWN, J.P.
"   T.PUGSLEY, J.P.   "   W.C.PHILLIPS.
"   M.MORDEY, J.P.   "   J.LISCOMBE, J.P.
"   T.GOLDSWORTHY, J.P.   "   F.PHILLIPS, J.P.
"   W.J.LLOYD, J.P.   "   T.PARRY, J.P.
COUNCILLOR F.P.ROBJENT.

ENGINEERS:
F.ARNODIN.   R.H.HAYNES.
CONTRACTOR: ALFRED THORNE.   TOWN CLERK: A.A.NEWMAN.

154—Plaque erected to commemorate the opening of the Transporter Bridge
12 September 1906.

155—Viscount Tredegar and other dignitaries at the opening of the Transporter
Bridge 1906.

156—The procession at the opening of the Transporter Bridge 1906. (West of England Tavern, Mill Parade in background.)

157—Lord Tredegar alights from the car after the first crossing.

158—The Transporter Bridge during construction about 1904.

159—The Bridge nearing completion. Photo taken 4 November 1905.

160—View from the top of the Bridge taken on 18 August 1959 showing Watchhouse Parade and part of south Pill.

161—The first Transporter Bridge built at Bilbao in 1889.

162—The car coming in to the west bank.

163—Steve Sims, Pill boxer, uses the steps of the Bridge for training. 1983.

164—Daniel Street from Alma Street looking towards Royal Gwent Hospital Entrance. April 1974 before demolition.

165—Albion Street from Frederick Street Bridge 1980. Before erection of Leisure Centre.

166—Commerical Road, near Albert Street during the Jazz Festival 1977.

167—George Street during reconstruction.

168—Lime Street from Mendalgief Road. November 1979.
Just before demolition.

169—Temple Street looking towards Commercial Road (Library on left, old Police Station on right). June 1977.

170—Pottery Terrace looking towards Alexandra Road November 1979.

171—Courtybella Street houses (on right) ready for demolition.
December 1979.

172—Dolphin Street showing environmental improvements May 1976.

Capel Crescent, P.

Adjoining Capel-street.

1 Williams Thos. fitter
2 Beasant E. engine driver
3 Waters John, guard
4 French W.H. shipwright
5 Parfitt G. railway police
6 Rosser Wm. baker
7 Lewis T. engine driver
8 Waters J. railway police
9 Hughes Thos. engineer
10 Roberts Wm. labourer
11 Westwood E. eng. driver
12 Hanham George, clerk
13 Green H. engine driver
14 Neighbour A. fireman
15 Baker Geo. engine driver
16 Baker Mrs. M. A.
17 Avons Jas. carpenter
18 Moore Hy. engine driver
19 Gomer Robt. mason
20 Jones Geo. G. smith
21 Musty Jos. inspector
22 Unbuilt
23 Hopkins H. storekeeper
24 Atherton Chas. H. guard
25 Pearce J. railway guard
26 Shute Chas. smith
27 Morgan Miss M. E.
28 Hughes John H. clerk

155

Temple Street, P.

From 132 Commercial-road.

1 Gilman Frank, fitter
2 Gorman Morris, labourer
3 Cousins Geo. mechanic
4 Bernier Alfd. shipwright
Trinity Boys' School
5 Reed Annie
6 Dawkins E. A. grocer
7 Richards Henry, smith
8 Warlow James, smith
9 Hughes Chas. labourer
Branch Police Station
10 Crowley M. coal trimmer
Moulton & Brownscombe
builders & contractors
(return.)
11 Payne Mrs. Ann
12 Cambray Harry, painter
13 James Herbert, smith
14 Pearce Thos. goods guard
15 Ferris E. railway police
16 Forest Wm. moulder
17 Waters Alfred, mason
18 Roberts Wm. guard
19 Morgan Wm. carpenter
20 Shea Richard, labourer
21 Bowen Henry, labourer
22 Cox Wm. fitter
23 Smith Mark, labourer
24 Cox Joseph, gardener
25 Triller Lucy
26 Tucker Mary Ann
27 Honeywill John, tailor
Site for new Reading Room
(Free Library)
Elliot Home for Seamen—
Wm. Dunn, supt.
Sailors' Church & Institute
Garry Rev. W. W. chaplaincy

173 & 174—Extracts from 1889 Directory showing names of residents in Capel Crescent and Temple Street.

175—The Old Town Dock mid 1800's.

176—Ships at the Old Town Dock mid/late 1800's.

177—Coal hoists at the Old Town Dock. Late 1800's.

178—Aerial view of North and South Docks. About 1920.

179—HRH Prince Arthur of Connaught on Lord Tredegar's Yacht.

180—"Liberty" at opening of new lock at Alexandra Docks 14 July 1914.

181—"Liberty" leaving South Dock after opening of lock 14 July 1914.

182—Aerial view of South Dock showing coal hoists about 1920.

183—The Commissioners Dredger "Usk".

184—Coal shipping at the Alexandra Docks.

185—Coal hoist at the Alexandra Dock 1912.

186—Alexandra Dock. Early 1900's.

187—Harbour Commisioners' vessel "Uskmoor" "retires" after 25 years service.
March 1983.

188—Newport Irish Rugby Team 1920 containing some of Pill's well known personalities.

Back Row: Reg Plummer (Referee), T Regan (Committee), W Broad, R Murphy, D McCarthy (Committee), W Casey (Chairman), E G Lyons, D Cashman (Committee). **Second Row:** J Collins, W Casey, H Huish, J Lenaham, J Whitfield, J Lynch, W O'Neil, M Morrissey (Treas), J Capel (Touch Judge). **Third Row:** W Cashman, Jerry Shea, Counc Peter Wright (Mayor), M Casey (Capt), Rev Fr Hickey, Rev Fr Cummings; M Mahoney. **Front Row:** F Watkins, W Shea, F Collins, M O'Connell.

189—Councillor Peter Wright.

190—Church House, Portland Street, where W H Davies spent his
early childhood.

191—W H Davies visits Church House in 1938 and is greeted by the Mayor Ald Mrs M A Hart of Lewis Street. Also in the photograph are the Poet Laureate (John Masefield), the Mayor's Secretary (Bryn Davies), and Mrs W H Davies.

192—Newport's first lady Mayor, Ald Mrs Mary Hart OBE JP signing the register in the Council Chamber, Town Hall, 9 November 1937.

Left to Right: Counc A E Wills JP, W H Robinson (Chief Constable), Mrs I C Vincent (Retiring Mayoress); Ald C T Clissitt JP, Ald Major I C Vincent (Retiring Mayor), Counc J R Wardell (Deputy Mayor 1937/38); Her Worship the Mayor Ald Mrs Hart; O Treharne Morgan (Town Clerk), Mr H J Hart, Mrs E W King (Retiring Deputy Mayoress).

193—Ald Mrs Hart being admitted to the Gorsedd in 1938.

194—Ald Mrs Hart in the Mayoral Procession passing St Paul's Church November 1937. (At the time when cinemas were popular and nearly everyone wore a hat!!!)

195—Ald Mrs Hart with Miss Gracie Fields on her visit to Newport in 1938.

196—The old National Schools opposite St Paul's Church where Mr J H Thomas received his early education. Late 1800's.

197—The Chemists Shop near to the William IV Public House where Mr Thomas worked as a lad, and a little further along Commercial Street, the National Schools.   Early 1900's.

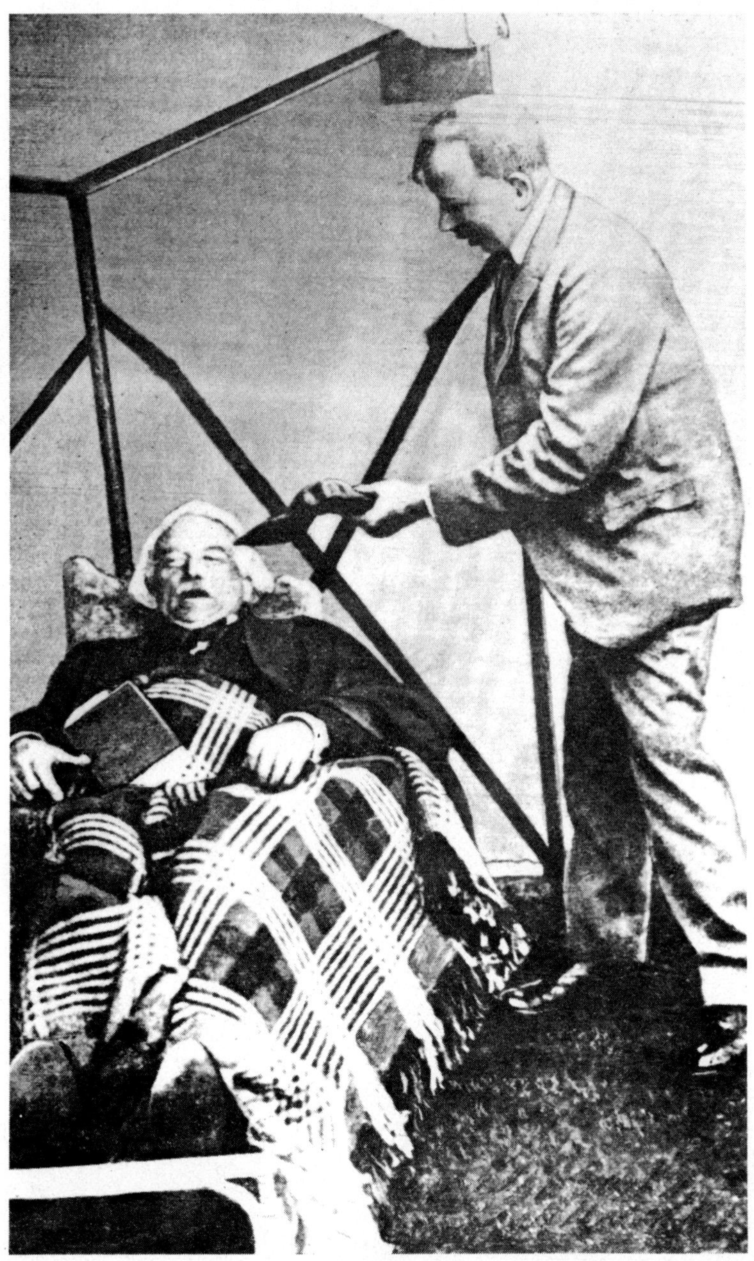

198—An informal snapshot from Mr Thomas's photographic album—a "passage of arms" between Mr Lloyd George and Mr Thomas.

199—The west wing wall trench looking north showing timbering before the collapse 13 June 1909.

200—The day of the tragedy showing the collapsed west wing wall trench, looking north. 2 July 1909.

201—The trench flooded July 1909.

202—The Rescue Team with Tom (Toya) Lewis on extreme right.

203—Pill YMCA RFC 1919-20 showing Mr W T Moore on extreme left back row.

Back Row: W T Moore (Chairman), W Carter, A Marshall, P Giblin, R Travers, G James. **Second Row:** T McGuire (Trainer), S Litson, R O Morris, L A Morris, F Nicholas, T Adams, J Rich, A Fountaine. **Front Row:** B Hurley, D Mulchay, C Short (Capt), J McCarthy, S V Fairfax (Sec).

204—Mr Moore meets the Prime Minister, Mr Clem Attlee and Mrs Attlee.

205—Opening of Temple Street YMCA Bazaar 1926, by the Mayor Arthur T W
James, Mr Moore in front row, fourth from the left.

206—Boys in the workshop of the Temple Street YMCA 1930's.

207—Jerry Shea.

208—Johnny Basham (on right).

209—Pill Harriers Cricket Team 1904.
Back Row: J E Webb, R H Smith, J Richards, J Spooner, G F Swallow. **Middle Row:** C Baldwin, T Iggulden, J Wesley-Paul, J Osborne, E V Swallow. **Front Row:** W Priest, F E Greenland.

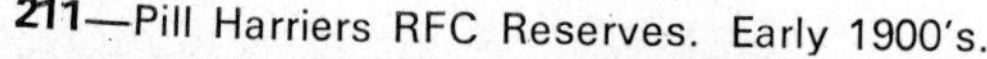

210—Pill Harriers Cricket Team. Early 1900's.

211—Pill Harriers RFC Reserves. Early 1900's.

212—Pill Harriers RFC 1906.

213—Pill Harriers Reserves 1911/12.
Back Row: J Hanbury, F Berry, F Jones (Vice-Capt), S Roberts, D Marshall, A Johnson, W Pearce, E Dyer, W Berry, J Yendal, W Robinson. **Middle Row:** W Griffin, J Jenkins, A Hoods, J Harris, A Morgan (Capt), F Taylor, T Bailey, B Lemerton, A Dart (Trainer). **Front Row:** F Morgan, T Radford, H Pring, A Pollock, R Pring.

214—Pill Harriers 1st XV 1912/13.

Back Row: G Merry (Trainer), W Radford, J Sharren, J Whitfield, T Corrigan, J Fairfax, J Casey, H Hathaway, E Dyer. **Middle Row:** G Armstrong, M Casey, F Watkins, W Curran, W Haley (Capt), R Carney (Vice-Capt), G Andrews, F Johnson. **Front Row:** S Manship, H Ritter, P Harding.

215—Pill Harriers Reserves 1912/13.

Back Row: F Berry, H Powell, C Davies, J Marshall, T Corrigan, J Whitfield, S Thomas, M Williams. **Middle Row:** C Cankett (Sec), B Davies, S Roberts, T Radford (Capt), G Cankett, J Heaven, W Hawen. **Front Row:** W Clissett, T Swadling, T Roberts, F Lucas, A Jones, H Pring, C Manship.

216—Pill Harriers RFC 1919.

217—Pill Harriers 1922.

Back Row: Trainer, M O'Brien, W Clark, W Davies, P Davies, Jackson, D Bale. **Middle Row:** W Richardson, H Rich, M Mitchell, J Roberts (Capt), R Osmond, J Clark, C Manley. **Front Row:** N Saysell, Watkins, J. Morgan.

218—Pill Harriers 1930.

Back Row: T Sinclair, G Manley, W Davies, R Griffiths, J Collins, G Gray, W Carter, R Osbourne, A Duncan, A Givvons. **Middle Row:** R Abraham, E Brown, W Lewis, L Travers, J Smith, M Doherty. **Front Row:** L Pritchard, H Gardner.

219—Two outstanding Welsh hookers—William (left) and George (right) Travers—father and son. William 12 caps (1937-49), George 25 caps (1903-11).

220—George (Torpie) Thompson a Pill bantamweight who won the "Sporting Chronicle" Gold Belt and as a rugby player represented Newport and Abertillery. "Torpie" is seen here with Elishah Attwell and his trainer Eddie. In front Arthur Fisher and George Thompson (Snr).

221—HMS Mutine Boxing Team 1927. Whole team consisted of Pill boxers.

222—George Settlerland another famous Pill boxer 1920's who still lives in Pill (302 Lewis Close).

223—St Joseph's Boxing Club 1980 (some names missing).

Back Row: B Hurley, M Holland, T McCorry, J Davies, R Chambers, C Byron **Fourth Row:** A Gordon, T Goulding, A Ali, A Torgesen, S Reily, R Chard, V Waite, M Byron. **Third Row:** B Byron, G Shorney, N Whelan, M Santini, S Tadman, G Gibbons, S Davies, R Chambers. **Second Row:** K Merret, C Merret, K Fletcher, C Hammond, F Hashi. **Front Row:** J Chambers, M Williams, R Davies. A Olsen.

224—Alexandra Dock Athletic Club 1923/24.

Back Row: J Davey, W Saysell, W Rees, A Pollard, A Cooper, P Davey, F Temple, W Burgess, A Pitman, F Harris, W Horn. **Third Row:** A Harris, Mr Thomas, C Weaver, W Gearon, S Fairfax, A St Clare, P Haslett, W Maloney (Chairman), W G Turner (Sec). **Second Row:** P Saysell (Trainer), T Watts, S Davies, A Simmonds, T Henson (Capt), D Rowe, W Stevens, H Llanfear. **Front Row:** G Thomas, G Southern, W Bowdler, A Bissex.

225—Clytha Villa Baseball Team. Winners of the Argus Cup. Early 1900's.

226—Clytha Villa Baseball Team 1926/27.

Inset: L Book (Sec), G Scott (President), R Attwell. **Back Row:** C Jones, R Clarke, A D Fairfax, F Manship, G Fisher. **Third row:** T Chapman, A Myles, S V Fairfax, J Rondel, G Rudd, G Morgan, F Berry, R S Herbert. **Second Row:** M Doherty, C Sheppard, Carl Gray, W Gray, C Berry. **Front Row:** T Woods, S. Jones.

227—Monmouthshire Baseball Team 1913.
Team includes Jack Wetter, Ebb Wetter, W Sears, Carl Gray and H Wreford.

228—Monmouthshire Baseball Team at Pill Grounds. About 1914.
Team includes Carl Gray, Fred Baker, Johna Clark, Spencer, Charles Sheppard, Alec Fountain,
Billy Iles, Jack Wetter and J Hillman.

229—Pill Harlequins Baseball Club 1923.

230—Clytha Villa Baseball Team 1930.

Back Row: G Tadman, A Roxburgh, T England, B Pritchard, M Cook, A Wood. **Middle Row:** B Clarke, C Woods, G Lyes, D Walsh, R Attewell, G Tasker, L Cook. **Front Row:** R Rudd, G Sheppard, G Thomas (Capt), J Clarke, C Berry. **Seated:** C Gray, W Gray.

231—Welsh Baseball Team at Cardiff Arms Park 1936.

Team includes Pill players Harry Gardner (seated on extreme left) and Reg St Clare, third from left.

232—Docks Athletic Baseball Team 1930.

Back Row: W Taylor, E O'Brien, John Howells, A Alonzi, Jack Barber, W Lyons, J Wren.
Middle Row: Bill Channing, Dick Marsh, G Fitzgerald, D Mahoney, T Smith, F Gibson.
Front Row: W Flanagan (Welsh Cap); J Brunnock, J Smith, C Samuels (Welsh Cap).

233—Another sporting father and son combination—Harry Gardner who had nine consecutive Welsh caps for baseball and his son Paul with five.

234—Munition Girls' Rugby Team during the first world war.

235—Newport Ladies' Rugby Team taken at their HQ—Pill Grounds.
Group includes Ebb Parry, Diksha Powell, Lena Osmond, Jim Yendall, Mr Trigg, Popsy Capell.
Played for charity during first world war.

236—One of Pill's sporting families — The Caseys, Bill Casey was also the Town's Mayor in 1935/36.

237—Pill Rovers RFC 1919/20. This team's HQ was "The Hastings" Pub in Commercial Road.

(Some names missing). **Back Row:** Bill Doughty, Albert Fryer, Gerry Shea, Jack Tucker, J Kellaher. **Middle Row:** H Walker, H Gibbin, C Short, J Haydon, Billy Friend, J Howells, J Cartwell. **Seated:** H Murphy, Channing. **Front Row:** E Duggan.

238—Pill United RFC. About 1920.

239—Pill Labour RFC 1973.

Back Row: R Williams, R Emms, R Evans, K Nicholas, A Taylor, R Williams, P Johnson, R Strawbridge (C.pt), R Collins, D Godwin, P Gardner, P Walters, L Nolan. **Front Row:** J Nichols, T Bartlett, C Lee, K Collins, D Davy, G Picton.

240—Spring Gardens OB Baseball Team 1931.

Back Row: B Thomas, A Periam, S Fenhers, M Thomas, H Herd, C Rogers. **Middle Row:** R Saunders, B Gough, T Davies, H Periam, W Booth. **Front Row:** A Taylor, C Pring, W Pippin.

241—St Michael's OB Baseball Team being presented with the Argus Cup 3 August 1953 (losing finalists—Pill Labour).

Left to Right: S Stoneman, B Mulchay, W MacNamara, J Murphy, J Fryer, D McCarthy, P Doherty, I Thomas, K Cook (Capt), A Nelson, E Delahay, "Topsy" Berry (Pill Labour), T Jenkins, J Brunnock (Pill Labour).

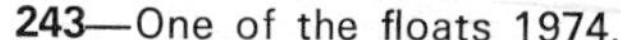

242—Festival and Carnival 1974. The Mayor Councillor John Marsh chats with the Temple Street children 1974.

243—One of the floats 1974.

244—Some Walking Entries for the Carnival 1974.

245—The Queen (Louise Wainfour) and her Court, Alison Collins, Barbara Frampton, Cindy Moore and Ruth McGuire. Also in the photograph are Councillor Aubrey Hames, Mr Roy Hughes MP, Alan Perry (Committee), George Bullock (Organising Secretary). 1974.

246—New Ruperra Street Tea Party 1974.

247—Staff of the Royal Gwent Hospital watch the Carnival go by. 1974.

248—Festival and Carnival 1975. The Queen and her Court on the Carnival Float 1975. Queen: Claire Hindman. Court: Jane Alpin, Jane Thomas, Helen Murray and Christine Osmond.

249—The Salvation Army Band play at the Open Air Sunday Service at Courtybella Green 1975.

250—One of the Jazz Bands marching down Commercial Road just after leaving the Cattle Market 1975.

251—One of the floats leaving the Docks 1975.

252—Festival and Carnival 1976. The Photographic Exhibition at the Pill Advice Centre 1976.

253—The Queen (Sylvia Burke) and her Court Ladies Helen Murray, Carrie Bird, Carol Murray and Karen Smith. Mr. Roy Hughes MP on left 1976.

254—The winners of the "I Spy" Competition with Councillor Alan Perry 1976.

255—The Festival Committee 1976.

Left to Right: Joan Wesson, Stan Casey, Mo Price, Stan Thomas, Marion Perry, Alan Perry, Iris Thomas, George French; Rene Metcalfe, Mervyn Jenkins, Jean Bird, Roy Maddocks, Pat Larder, Cecil Meadows, Dorothy Williams, Cynthia Johnson.

255A—David Pearce, British Heavyweight Champion from September 1983. This photo taken in 1978 when he became a professional boxer.

256—Temple Street Branch Library in 1983.

257—The Author (Cliff Knight) chats to the Library Assistant Mary Rowland at Temple Street Library.

258—Carved headstone 1889 at Temple Street Library (photo taken 1983).